*M*ystifying *M*ind *R*eading *T*ricks

ROBERT MANDELBERG

Illustrated by Ferruccio Sardella

STERLING PUBLISHING CO., INC.
New York

To Nika, my partner in mind reading and in life.

My thanks to Lori Horak for her encouragement, Peter Gordon for sharing some of his closely guarded mind reading secrets, and Michael Brown for helping to perfect "The Name Game."

Library of Congress Cataloging-in-Publication Data

Mandelberg, Robert.
  Mystifying mind reading tricks / Robert Mandelberg.
    p.   cm.
  Includes index.
  ISBN 0-8069-8811-8
    1. Magic tricks. 2. Telepathy. I. Title.

GV1553.M35 2002
793.8—dc21   2002066866

Edited by Peter Gordon

2 4 6 8 10 9 7 5 3 1

Published by Sterling Publishing Company, Inc.
387 Park Avenue South, New York, N.Y. 10016
© 2002 by Robert Mandelberg
Distributed in Canada by Sterling Publishing
C/o Canadian Manda Group, One Atlantic Avenue, Suite 105
Toronto, Ontario, Canada M6K 3E7
Distributed in Great Britain and Europe by Chris Lloyd at Orca Book
Services, Stanley House, Fleets Lane, Poole BH15 3AJ, England
Distributed in Australia by Capricorn Link (Australia) Pty. Ltd.
P.O. Box 704, Windsor, NSW 2756 Australia

Sterling ISBN 0-8069-8811-8

Contents

Introduction

Ah, if only I had a dollar for every time someone looked at me in awe and said, "How did you *do* that?" It's simpler and more spectacular than magic; more enticing than card tricks; much more fun than sleight of hand. What is it? It is the illusion that I am actually reading people's minds.

At parties, someone will invariably gather together a group of people and bring me over to "read minds." Although by now I am quite used to spectators' reactions when I correctly guess what they are thinking, it never grows tiresome. Admittedly, it is great fun to be challenged by a skeptic, only to leave him sitting in a chair, dumbfounded, mouth agape, wondering how I *did* that.

Are these tricks? Well, it is certainly true that there is some deception involved; however, it is more appropriate to refer to them as demonstrations since a great number of people are convinced that I possess supernatural mental powers. The truth is I have a hard time operating a yo-yo.

After performing these entertaining demonstrations for my friends, family, and acquaintances for the past ten years, I have decided to share them so that others can enjoy the fun and excitement of mind reading. In this book, you will find a collection of the most extraordinary, fascinating, and spellbinding mind reading exhibitions ever created—guaranteed to amaze and delight any audience!

You will learn not only the secrets of these incredible feats, but also how to use them effectively to maximize their impact. Most of the fun in performing and witnessing these exercises is the build-up and mystique that leads to the demonstration.

The best part is that these crowd-pleasers are so simple to master. Once you learn the basics, a little practice and touch of showmanship will make you the hit of any party. This book will describe, in detail, how to perform a wide variety of demonstrations both independently and with the aid of a partner.

Are you ready to begin?

Yes?

I knew it!

How did I *do* that?

—Robert Mandelberg

The Mystique of Mind Reading

1

Mind reading ... the thought of it is so alluring, so mystical; it always has been. If you asked 100 people at random what super-human power they would most like to possess, what do you think it would be?

Well, it would probably be to live forever—but a close second would surely be ... the ability to go back in time (that's my personal favorite—I've always wanted to meet Abraham Lincoln). My point is that somewhere behind x-ray vision, flying, being invisible, and making gold out of water would be the magical, elusive, and awe-inspiring ability to read minds.

It is the one ability that is missing from our nearly perfect reper-toire of senses. I would gladly trade one of my other senses to be able to know what someone is thinking. Smell, for instance. Do we really need smell? If you're honest like I am, I think you'd admit that most of the things we smell on a day-to-day basis are unpleas-ant anyway. That is not to say that other people's thoughts would be any less unpleasant.

Although this book will not teach you to be clairvoyant, it will provide you with all of the secrets and information you need to give the illusion that you have the power to read minds. And you don't have to give up your sense of smell to do it!

You have in your hands a powerful tool. I have selected, modi-fied, and embellished the *very best* mind reading demonstrations ever created. What you are about to learn is the cream of the crop in mind reading. I am not filling this book with hundreds of bland, semi-amusing tricks. No. I wouldn't do that to you. I have too much respect for you. Instead, I will present only a handful of top-quality, high-impact demonstrations—guaranteed to leave your audience flabbergasted.

By the way, you've probably realized that soon I will run out of synonyms for the word "amazed." As you can see, we are only in Chapter 1 and I've already had to resort to "flabbergasted."

Be Strong

With this extraordinary power I am about to bestow upon you comes significant responsibility. The most difficult part of performing these demonstrations is not revealing the secret of how they are accomplished. When friends and family members begin insisting on learning the answer, you must stick to your guns and keep silent.

The reason is simple: The audience's amazement will quickly dissipate and turn to scorn and disappointment. Many times, once these so-called friends of yours learn the secret to a demonstration, they will have the nerve to deny the sheer brilliance of the feat. You will hear words to the effect of: "Oh, yeah, I figured it was something like that." Believe me, it is much better to leave them awestruck and upset than unimpressed and smug. (I hate smug.)

Beware of shameful begging. Have you ever seen a grown man beg? Let me warn you: It isn't pretty. One of the more unfortunate aspects of being able to perform these demonstrations successfully is that begging is an inevitable part of the process. It goes like this:

The audience is mesmerized by a particularly entertaining mind reading demonstration. Among the "Wow"s and "That's amazing!"s and "I'm flabbergasted"s, there is always at least one audience member who *must* know how the demonstration was performed. At first he or she will casually ask you for the secret. Despite your refusal to cooperate, the question is repeated. "No, really, how did you *do* that?" Several more refusals lead to more insistence that you divulge the answer.

It is what I call the five stages of mind amazement, or if you prefer, flabbergastedness:

Denial ... shock ... anger ... compromise ... and finally, acceptance.

Do I mind when people beg me like this? Of course not! I remember what it was like. You see, this is how I learned the secret

8

of many of these demonstrations. Begging can be quite effective. So, you must be strong and not give in!

History of Mind Reading

Although mind reading demonstrations have existed for many centuries, it is difficult to find recorded evidence of these phenomena. One of the earliest mind reading feats ever documented was performed by Jean Eugene Robert-Houdin in France in the 19th century. This immensely talented illusionist was regarded as the best magician of his time. Does his name sound familiar? Well, it should. It is said that Houdini (né Erich Weiss) chose his stage name in honor of this great performer.

Deep in the heart of the Loire Valley in France, there is a museum devoted to the magic of Jean Eugene Robert-Houdin. La Maison de la Magie (the House of Magic) features a complete history of his career as well as some of the props that he used in his act. It was here that I learned about the demonstration that Robert-Houdin performed with his young son. It went like this:

Robert-Houdin would announce to the crowd that his son was capable of reading minds. To prove this, he led his son to a chair on stage and blindfolded him. Mr. Robert-Houdin would then approach a member of the audience and ask for a personal item.

Once he received the item, he would hold it up to show the audience. Then he would ring a bell and ask his son what the item was. Even though his son was blindfolded, he would predict it correctly each time.

How was this demonstration performed? Well, the answer is not documented, but many suspect that Robert-Houdin was giving his son signals by using the bell. Just imagine all the practice that would be required to master this system. There are many common personal items that audience members would carry with them—perhaps a watch, a hat, a wallet, etc. These items can all be associated with certain bell signals.

It is probable that the way the father rang the bell would indicate which item was selected. It is also likely that Robert-Houdin influenced audience members to produce certain personal articles in order to make the predicting easier.

The method of using a partner to transmit signals will be discussed in great detail later in this book. You will see that although there are many variations, the premise of sending secret codes to an accomplice is present in many demonstrations. The effectiveness of these feats is solely dependent upon how well the performers succeed in concealing their codes.

Throughout this book, I will be referring many times to your "audience." This does not necessarily have to be 25,000 people packed into an arena to see "You the Great" perform an evening full of mind-numbing feats. For many of these demonstrations, your audience can simply consist of just your neighbor or your milkman or the woman behind the counter at the 7-Eleven. (Who knows, you may even get a free Slurpee out of it!)

2

Presentation Is Key

The Art of "Selling" the Demonstration to the Audience

*"A magician is merely an actor ...
an actor playing the part of a magician."*
—Jean Eugene Robert-Houdin

How true the above statement is! And the same applies to a mind reader. One of the most important aspects of mind reading is selling it to the audience. In the next several chapters, you will not only discover the secret to some brain-jolting demonstrations, but you will also learn how to perform them with flair and style.

There are basically two ways you can play your part. The first is with humor using a lighthearted, comedic approach. In many of these demonstrations you will have great fun "hamming it up."

If comedy is not your style, then you can try a more somber attitude, as if you are truly performing great feats of mentalism. If you play this part effectively, you will have some of your audience convinced that you are indeed a mind reader.

You doubt me? Please, skeptical reader, do not underestimate the gullibility of your fellow humans. Even if audience members claim that they know some sort of trick is involved, deep down in their hearts they are never really 100% sure. After all, some of these demonstrations are just so baffling that if you acted your part correctly you will "freak out" some of the spectators. In some circles, it would not be uncommon to hear, "Stop that, dude, you are totally freaking me out." That is a compliment. I think.

After each demonstration is explained, there will be a section entitled *Tips & Techniques*. These sections are packed with helpful hints that provide performance suggestions and ideas to enhance the impact of the demonstration.

Tips & Techniques

See? This chapter has one too.

If you are interested in establishing a serious, mystical atmosphere for your demonstrations, there are several steps you can take.

Proper lighting is very effective. Turning off all lights and using candles will set the mood for a touch of wizardry or something in the style of Rod Serling. You can play some soft New Age music in the background and even burn some incense.

Virtually anything is acceptable. You can insist on complete silence, or to add a touch of mystery have the audience repeat a simple chant.

The approach I usually prefer is comedic in nature. If you have a little showmanship in your bones, you can leave your audience both mystified and hysterical. If this is how people usually react to you, then you may not notice the difference.

The techniques you can use to inject humor into your presentation can range from subtle comments to outlandish displays of silliness.

On several occasions I appeared at business and social functions as a comedic mind reader, Sahib the Fortune Teller. My entire routine consisted of a handful of demonstrations you will be reading about in later chapters. "Sahib" would be dressed in a hodgepodge of mismatched, ludicrous, pseudo-Gypsy clothing styles. My partner acted as my faithful and humble assistant who walked a few feet in front of me, sweeping my upcoming path with a broom as I strolled from table to table.

Sahib had a real attitude problem. He was surly, obnoxious, and sarcastic—but outrageously funny. This bizarre persona added an entirely new dimension to these mind reading demonstrations.

If dressing as Sahib the Fortune Teller is a bit too far-fetched for your conservative tastes, then you may want to opt for a more conventional approach. You can still use comedy without dressing like an outcast.

It is always fun to lead into each demonstration with a preposterous story. The wackier the better! Don't be afraid to mention how you learned a particular demonstration in an earlier life from a blind, mute monk in Katmandu on a Tuesday, late in September of 1373.

As you begin to perfect these demonstrations, you can customize each feat according to your personality. Feel free to vary the presentation and technique as long as the final outcome remains constant.

What I am trying to say is that you should use your creativity to make these feats as fun as possible—for yourself and for your audience. In each chapter, I will present suggestions on how you can inject showmanship into your performance.

Warm-Up

When you first begin talking to your audience about mind reading, you can mention that, to some degree, each and every one of us has a certain amount of ESP. It is a matter of harnessing the talent and learning how to use it.

Continue to explain that you have a simple test that you would like to conduct to see if someone truly has ESP. At this point, produce a sealed envelope and hold it out in front of you. Select someone in your audience and say the following:

"I have written a word on a piece of paper in this envelope. Tell me, do you know what that word is?"

Well, it has been my experience that nine times out of ten the person will say "No." At that point, you rip open the envelope, unfold the paper, and show the audience that the person you select-ed does indeed have ESP, because on the paper written in large, thick, black magic marker is the word "No."

This usually generates laughter and is a good lead-in to the "real" mind reading exhibitions. What happens if they say something other than no? I generally tell them they were not concentrating and try someone else in the audience. Eventually someone will say "No."

Cheating

This is a sensitive subject because most of you, like myself, have been brought up with the notion that cheating is wrong. I implore you to forget everything your parents ever taught you about right or wrong. Mind reading is anarchy. It is a deceitful, sneaky, and dia-bolical way of life. Accept it.

To perform any effective mind reading demonstration, you must deceive your audience one way or another. Usually it is by dis-creetly giving secret codes to a partner, but sometimes other forms of treachery are employed.

Please don't think me evil. I only mention this because you need to understand that your only goal is to make the demonstration work! I will teach you all the techniques necessary to perform these feats flawlessly. But—and this is important—if you can get the answer quicker by cheating and using a shortcut, feel free to do so.

For example: You are performing a demonstration where your partner knows the secret answer and is giving you hidden clues. Using this method, it will take a few moments for you to decipher the message. If your audience becomes distracted (sometimes you can cause this), there is no harm in your partner whispering or pointing or "mouthing" the answer to speed things along. The faster you reveal the secret answer, the greater the impact.

When appropriate, I will suggest techniques that you can use to "cheat" or circumvent the "honest" mind reading procedures to speed things along. If you decide to use any of these methods, please be sure of one thing: *Do not get caught!*

Now that we are beginning to understand each other, I think that we can proceed to the actual mind reading demonstrations.

Mind Reading Demonstrations

In the pages to follow, I have described—in detail—thirteen entertaining and dazzling mind reading demonstrations. Some are very simple to perform and others require considerable setup or practice. Before each description, I have included a chart that rates the demonstration in several areas.

Rating System

DIFFICULTY LEVEL: ◆◆◆◆◆

If you want to see how easy the demonstration is to perform, check this rating. A low score (two diamonds or less out of five) means that most people who are bright enough to read this book probably have what it takes to perform the demonstration successfully. A score of more than three diamonds indicates that the demonstration requires skill, setup, or rehearsal to be performed effectively. The highest difficulty rating is five diamonds.

IMPACT: ✹✹✹✹✹

When performed correctly, each demonstration discussed in this book will make an impression on the audience. Some of these demonstrations are designed to be simple icebreakers while others will have much more dramatic impact.

To see a demonstration's potential impact on an audience, check this rating. If the score is one or two stars, consider using this as a warm-up. Save the higher rated demonstrations for when you really want to shock your audience. The highest impact rating is five stars.

PARTNER

Some demonstrations will require the use of a partner and others can be performed independently. It is a good idea to train several people as partners to increase your chances of someone being available for impromptu demonstrations.

The partner's role is generally not very complicated, but vital for many feats described in this book. You will find it quite worthwhile to share these secrets with a few close friends so that they can help you in your performances.

PREPARATION

I have indicated the extent of the preparation required for each demonstration. In most feats involving a partner, some rehearsal is necessary to learn an easy code system. Don't panic. Most of these codes can be mastered with minimal practice; others require more time.

At times you will need to prepare a few simple props—paper, pencils, cards, etc. Many items that are required for these demonstrations are readily available in most homes.

Let's now take a look at some specific examples:

The One-Up Principle

This spectacular and remarkably simple technique is one of the oldest and most effective mind reading principles used by both amateur and professional performers alike. Master this technique and you will leave your friends and family speechless.

In the next few chapters you will learn some fun and innovative examples of the One-Up (or One-Ahead) Principle. Each demonstration is unique, but uses the same concept of staying one ahead of the audience.

*O*ne *A*head

4

DIFFICULTY LEVEL: ◆◆◆◆◆
IMPACT: ✳✳✳✳✳
PARTNER: NO
PREPARATION: NONE

Overview

As much as it pains me, you are about to learn the secret to my personal favorite demonstration. I do not mind confessing that I find it quite difficult to share this with you. You see, many of my friends have been pestering me for years to reveal this secret, and I have refused. My own mother doesn't know how it is done. Now I have to find a way to keep her out of the bookstore.

The Premise

Step 1: The mind reader places three small slips of paper and a pen on a table. He asks a member of the audience to think of a person's name, but not to reveal it. The mind reader then silently writes a prediction on a slip of paper, folds it up, and places it on the table—without anyone seeing what was written. The audience member then reveals the secret name he was thinking.

Step 2: The mind reader then asks a second member of the audience to think of a secret number and, again, not to reveal it. The audience member thinks of the number while the mind reader writes a prediction on another slip of paper. The mind reader folds the paper and places it on the table next to the first paper. The folded papers are *still not shown to the audience.* The audience member then reveals the secret number.

17

Step 3: Finally, this process is repeated once more, only this time the mind reader asks a third audience member to think of a color—either black or white. Again the mind reader writes a prediction, folds the paper, and places it on the table next to the other two. The audience member then reveals his color selection.

Step 4: A fourth audience member is asked to unfold the pieces of paper and read the predictions aloud. To the astonishment of the spectators, the answers are deadly accurate.

How is this possible? How did the mind reader know what the audience members were thinking? It's easy! Read on and see how simple the One-Up Principle is to master!

The Solution

You, as the mind reader, ask the first subject to think of a name. As detailed in the overview, when the subject indicates that he has selected a name, you pick up the pen and a slip of paper and begin to write. The audience is under the impression that you are predicting the secret name, but you're not. Instead, on the first piece of paper, you write down a color (either back or white). Without anyone seeing what was written down, the paper is folded and placed on the table.

Are you following me so far? Have you figured out how this works yet?

Now that the audience is satisfied that you have made a prediction and written it down, it is safe for the subject to reveal the secret name to you and the spectators. Here is where the One-Up Principle comes in:

In the next part of the demonstration, the second audience member is asked to think of a number. Instead of predicting a number, you write down the secret name! (Remember, no one will see what was written on the slips of paper until the end of the demonstration.) And how do you know what the secret name is? Simple! The first subject just revealed it!

The first subject thought it was safe to say the secret name— after all, you had already made your prediction and folded up the piece of paper. Little did the subject realize that you wrote your

18

prediction of the color, just to get him to reveal the name. (You're so devious!)

Okay, so let's play out the rest of the demonstration:

The second slip of paper (which contains the secret name) is folded and placed on the table. The subject then reveals the secret number—of course, believing that it is safe to do so.

I think you can see where this is going. While the third subject is thinking of a color—either black or white—what do you think you will be writing on the third slip of paper? Yes! The secret number!

This slip of paper is then folded and placed with the others. When the slips of paper are unfolded and the answers are revealed, it appears as if you have predicted them accurately.

To illustrate the order of your predictions, see the chart below:

Paper	What they think you're writing	What you're actually writing
First slip	Name	Color
Second slip	Number	Name
Third slip	Color	Number

Well? What do you think? Spectacular?

By using the One-Up Principle, you stayed one step ahead of the audience the entire time!

Preparation

It's easy: Cut or tear three slips of paper and place them on a table. Since this demonstration can be performed without a partner, no rehearsal is necessary.

Tips & Techniques

- To make this demonstration even more sensational, encourage the audience members to make their secret selections as obscure as possible. A nice, long build-up prepares the audience for something extraordinary. For the secret name, you might tell the subject something like:

    Select a name that you would never normally think of. Don't pick "Joe" or "John" or my name, because if I guess it correctly, you will say it was too easy. Please, don't make it easy! Make it as hard as possible! It doesn't have to be just a first name; in fact, it could be a first, middle, and last name. It could be a foreign name for all I care. It doesn't even have to be a real name! It could even be "Schmaloopie Maloopie!" Whatever name you come up with, no matter how weird, I will guess what it is. And don't try using "Schmaloopie Maloopie!"

By leading up to the prediction in this manner, the subject is more likely to select an "impossible-to-guess" name. What do you care what it is? The subject will reveal it before you have to write it down!

- For the second part of the demonstration, you could try leading up to it as follows:

"Now I would like you to select a number between one and ten ... No, on second thought, that might be too easy. Maybe we should make it between 1 and 100 ... No, on second thought, I think that is still too easy. I'll tell you what: How about you think of a number between one and infinity, *fractions included!* And please, don't hold back; make it as impossible as you want!"

Wow, can you imagine the look on their faces when they see that you have accurately guessed 4,093,398¾?

- When a subject reveals a particularly unusual name or a crazy number, I usually remark, "Oh, that was a simple one. Everyone says that."

By now you have probably realized that there is a slight snag in this demonstration. How are you supposed to know whether to guess black or white for the color? That's a good question! How will you know? After all, you're not really a mind reader!

It's a 50-50 guess. There is no perfect solution, but there are a couple of techniques that I have used to increase my chances of predicting it correctly.

- First, you can attempt to influence the desired answer. When you reach the color portion of the demonstration, insist that the audience member think of a color (black or white) immediately, as soon as you pose the question. Then, say the first color softly and the other color with more emphasis. You can say something like:

"Now I would like you to think of an answer as soon as I clap my hands. Are you ready? Think of a color, either black or WHITE. [clap]" Many times, the subject will select "white" when presented this way. Of course, you don't want to make it too obvious.

- Another method that I have found to be effective is changing the colors to reflect the subject's personality. When my subject is male, I often ask that he choose between a masculine and feminine color, such as pink or blue. Many men will opt for blue.

- Sometimes I will change the color selections depending upon the situation. For example, if the subject is dressed entirely in red, I will use that as one of the choices.

- Keep in mind that even if you select the wrong color, this demonstration is still remarkable. In a worst-case scenario, you will get *two out of three answers correct!* That is incredible! And the one you missed was the simplest of all! I mean, if you manage to predict Schmaloopie Maloopie as the name and 4,093,398¾ as the number, do you really think that the audience will make a big deal because you couldn't guess black or white? Hardly.

When this happens to me, I generally remark, "Well, I would have predicted this one correctly, but I'm color blind." Okay, not terribly amusing, but it does the trick.

Often, when the color is predicted incorrectly, I hear the subject say "Oh! I was going to say black, but then I changed my mind at the last second!"

- Looking for a foolproof way to predict the color correctly? I have a technique that works flawlessly. Instead of writing your predictions on slips of paper, use index cards. And here is why: Before entering the performance room, you write the word "black" on an index card and place it in your front pocket.

You are then ready to begin the demonstration for your audience. When it is time to make your first prediction, write the word "white" on an index card and place it in your pocket. So, at this point, you will have two index cards in your pocket. One that says "black" and one that says "white." The audience, however, thinks you only have one

21

card in your pocket at this point. You will then proceed with the demonstration as described above. When you write your predictions to the other questions on the two remaining index cards, place them *between* the index cards that are already in your pocket. This way the index cards with the colors written on them are sandwiching the other predictions.

When it comes time to reveal your answers, simply put your hand in your pocket and remove the three correct predictions, leaving the fourth card in your pocket. If the subject says that "white" is the selected color, you will pull out the first three cards in your pocket. If the answer is "black," you remove the last three. The only tricky part of this technique is remembering which card is first.

- Instead of using three slips of paper, you may want to consider cutting a fourth. This extra slip of paper would be used to write the answers down after the subjects have revealed them. This "solution sheet" may come in handy in the case of hard to remember names or long numbers. You can discreetly glance at the sheet and then write your prediction on the appropriate slip of paper.

- After the predictions have been made, you will then have to select a person to open and read the slips of paper. There are two things to be careful of here. The first is that the subject cannot be allowed to open up the slips of paper in the order they were placed on the table. This would expose you for the fake you are. Instead, casually mix the slips of paper up as you shuffle them to the subject who will be reading them. Tell the subject that they can be opened in any order.

The second concern is that audience members get very suspicious if the mind reader starts to handle the slips of paper. You do have to "shuffle" the papers to a spectator to mix them up, but do not touch them with your hands. Use a pen and do it very slowly, or else you will be accused of substituting a slip of paper (audience members can be so paranoid!).

- Sometimes, at a party, when I am shuffling the pieces of paper to a subject to be read, and I know that I guessed all three correctly, I will get up and walk away. It is fun to leave the scene and just listen to their reactions from the next room as they open the slips of paper and wonder how it was done. Usually within a few minutes, I am hunted down and brought back into the room to perform the demonstration again (and again and again).

- A word of caution: It is entirely possible that audience members can solve this demonstration. If it is performed repeatedly, it is just a matter of time before someone guesses the solution. This is especially true if you get the color wrong. My advice is to limit this demonstration to just one performance. Chances are that nobody will figure it out.

- Although this demonstration is ideal for small groups, it can also be performed for an audience of one. Simply have the subject select all three secret answers, and open the slips after the predictions have been written. The concept is exactly the same.

- As with any of the demonstrations, presentation is key. One thing you can do to make the demonstration more enjoyable for the audience is to use some showmanship. While the subject is thinking of a name or number, you should be intently staring into the eyes of the subject, as if that will tell you what the person is thinking. An intense look and prolonged gaze will either appear amusing or spooky. Both work.

- If you are close with the audience, you can be a little more intimate. Pretend that you have to do bizarre things to predict the answers correctly. Placing your hand on the subject's head, or analyzing the back of the hand, or perhaps even sniffing the subject in odd places will create the impression that you are either psychic or psychotic. Again, both work.

Variations

Undoubtedly, you will be asked to perform this demonstration repeatedly. It is a lot of fun to perform but the odds of someone figuring it out increase significantly every time you do it. And remember, it is not a good idea to reveal the secret—no matter how much they beg—because it is never as impressive to the audience once they know how it is performed.

If you do decide to repeat this demonstration or would like to try a little variety, there are many ways you can alter the secret clues. Instead of predicting names, numbers, and colors, use your imagination and try different categories. After all, the process is exactly the same. The subjects will give you the answer before you write it down. Here is a list of suggestions for new categories, but feel free to make them up as you go along:

- Questions that relate only to the subject: What is the name of your third grade teacher or the first person you ever kissed? (Hopefully this will not be the same person.) Other examples can include:

    What is your middle name? Where were you born? Who is your favorite president? What was the name of your best friend in high school? What is your favorite television show? How much do you weigh? (Be careful with that one!)
- You can also ask more generic information such as:

    Name a place (could be a country, a state, or even a street address), a football player, a day on the calendar, a card out of the deck, etc.
- Another favorite category that I like to use is guessing how much money a subject has in his wallet, or what his driver's license number is. It is very effective and humorous when you predict something that the subject doesn't even know. Basically it does not matter what it is that you

24

are guessing. As long as the answer is given *before* you write your next prediction, any name, number, or other secret will work perfectly.

A Great Variation

Mathematical questions are *incredible!* Have one person in the audience conceive a very complex mathematical equation. Explain to this subject that he only has to create the problem—but not worry about finding the answer. Allow this person to write down the equation, because it will most likely be too long to remember. An example might be: 2,939,393 × 334,221,232.9809 × 4.2. When the subject has written down the equation, you ask him to read it to you. You then think about it for two seconds and write down your prediction (as if it were so simple to figure out!). You place the prediction folded in a piece of paper on the table.

Then have someone in the audience use a calculator to figure out the real answer. This answer is then written on another piece of paper just for reference (ostensibly to match it with your answer later, but really for you to be able to copy from during the next part of the demonstration).

Using the One-Up Principle, you didn't really write down the answer to the mathematical equation. Instead, you wrote either *Black* or *White.* During the next part of the demonstration, when you are supposed to be writing down your prediction to another question, you will discreetly write the math answer on the second slip of paper.

The audience will not only think that can you read minds, but your mental power is so potent, you can actually calculate 15-digit equations in a matter of seconds. Is there no end to your talent?

5

Bottom Dealer

DIFFICULTY LEVEL: ✦✦✦✦✦

IMPACT: ✸✸✸✸✸

PARTNER: NO

PREPARATION: NONE

The Premise

This mind reading trick is another example of the One-Up Principle:

The mind reader will guide the audience into selecting certain cards out of the deck—as if the audience members possess telepathic powers! As the demonstration begins, the mind reader fans a deck of cards *face down* on a table. She asks an audience member to point to a particular card—let's say the nine of hearts. The audience member takes a wild guess and points to a card that he believes

is the nine of hearts. (After all, how in the world would he know where the nine of hearts is—when the cards are still face down?)

The mind reader removes this card from the deck, making sure to keep it face down. She then peeks at this card and exclaims that the audience member was correct—still not showing the audience the card. The mind reader then asks another audience member to select the three of spades.

The second audience member surveys the deck and points to a card, taking another wild guess. The mind reader removes this card from the deck and takes a quick peek at it, making sure that no one else can see the card. Again, she announces that the subject has selected the correct card.

Finally, the mind reader says that she will select the final card herself, a four of diamonds. She then pulls a card from the deck and places it with the other two that have previously been selected. These three cards are then given to a fourth audience member who then reads them to a gasping, open-mouthed, delirious, begging-to-know-the-solution crowd.

The Solution

The solution to this demonstration is exactly the same as in Chapter 4. As you thoroughly shuffle the cards, you glance to see what the bottom card is before fanning the deck face down on a table. *Knowing this card is the key to the entire demonstration.*

For this example, let us assume that the bottom card was the nine of hearts. At the beginning of the demonstration, you announce that it is the audience who will be exhibiting their ESP skills. Once a spectator is selected, he is asked to point to the nine of hearts. You know that the nine of hearts is the bottom card, but you say nothing as the subject points to a card in the middle of the deck.

You then remove the selected card from the deck, making sure that no one sees what it is. After glancing at the card and seeing that it is the three of spades, you say that the nine of hearts has indeed been selected.

Let's put the One-Up Principle into effect. You now say that you need another member of the audience to select a different card. Hmm ... what card shall it be? I know! Let's try the three of spades!

Well, we know very well that the second audience member cannot possibly pick the three of spades, since it is in your hand already! The second audience member randomly selects another card, wrongly, of course, but it really doesn't matter! You remove it from the deck and glance at it, noticing that it is the four of diamonds. So now, you are holding two cards: the three of spades and the four of diamonds—although the audience has been told that it is the nine of hearts and three of spades.

To complete the demonstration, you then announce that you will personally select the last card. You pretend to make up a card at random. Can you guess what it is? Yes, the four of diamonds. Of course, the four of diamonds is already in your hand. In fact, the only card that has been called that is *not* in your hand is the nine of hearts. And we all know where that card is: at the bottom of the deck.

You then reach over to the deck to select the "four of diamonds," and which card will you choose? Yes! The bottom card—the nine of hearts.

Now you are holding three cards in your hand: The nine of hearts, the three of spades, and the four of diamonds. And these are the same three that have just been called.

This demonstration is an effective variation of the One-Up Principle, and can be used to follow "One Ahead."

Tips & Techniques

• What happens if the first spectator selects the card on the bottom of the deck? Is the demonstration ruined? Hardly. In fact, if you should ever happen to be so lucky, it will appear as if you are the greatest mind reader ever born. Just imagine: you ask the spectator to point to the nine of hearts when all of the cards are *face down*, and he actually gets it correct! All you have to do is simply turn the card over and show the audience that the spectator did indeed select the correct card.

Before doing this, however, you may want to ham it up just a bit, and savor this tidbit of incredibly good luck. Prior to looking at and revealing the card that was selected, you may want to get assurances from each audience member that if the card the spectator selected is indeed the nine of hearts, that this would be the most amazing demonstration ever. Do you like to gamble? This would be a good time to place a few bets that the card is what you say it is.

Of course, if this does happen, do not try to repeat this demonstration. How can it possibly turn out any better?

• By the way, the same principle applies if the second spectator should happen to pick the bottom card. Actually, it is even more miraculous that two audience members accurately selected two random cards.

• When the mind reader asks spectators to select specific cards, they are often a bit reluctant about trying it, because they are so sure that they will be wrong. Assure them that you have great confidence in them and that if they concentrate, they will surely select the correct card. After you peek at the card they selected and announce that it is correct, the audience generally reacts with disbelief and laughter. That is fine. We will see who is laughing when the cards are revealed.

Take Heart

DIFFICULTY LEVEL: ✦✦✦✦✦
IMPACT: ✻✻✻✻✻
PARTNER: NO
PREPARATION: NONE

Overview

In "Bottom Dealer," the mind reader has to get involved in the demonstration by selecting the last card himself. This takes away from the impact. Can you imagine how effective the demonstration would be if the mind reader never had to select a card? This would mean that the audience randomly chose all of the cards by themselves.

The Premise

This is exactly what happens in "Take Heart." In this demonstration, the mind reader uses only one suit. As an example, let's use hearts. Once the 13 hearts have been extracted from the deck, they are thoroughly mixed and then fanned *face down* on a table. In "Take Heart," the mind reader does not have to memorize the bottom card.

The beginning of this demonstration is the same as in "Bottom Dealer." A spectator is asked to point to a specific card. Once this is done, the mind reader glances at it, and then asks another spectator to select a different card.

Another audience member is selected to write down each card on a piece of paper as it is mentioned. This will come in handy at the end of the demonstration.

The process of selecting cards is repeated several more times. The mind reader then turns over the cards that were chosen one by one. To the astonishment of the audience, the cards match the ones that were called *in the exact order in which they were chosen.*

The Solution

After the cards are fanned out face down on a table, you arbitrarily select one of the hearts and ask a spectator to point to it. Let's again use the nine of hearts as an example. Chances are that the spectator will point to a card other than the nine of hearts. As in the prior demonstration, you will feign joyous surprise and announce that the correct card had been chosen.

For the sake of this explanation, let's say that the subject pointed to the ten of hearts. You then ask a second spectator to point to the card that she thinks is the ten of hearts. Each time a card is selected, it is put in a pile face down. The same process is repeated until the nine of hearts is selected by one of the audience members. As I stated above, another spectator writes down each card mentioned on a piece of paper.

Once the nine has been chosen, it is time to reveal the cards. Because the cards have been put in a pile in the order they were selected, they will match what the spectator has written on the piece of paper. The only exception to this is the nine of hearts, which is now on the top of the deck. This is not good—we need the nine to be on the bottom of the deck. Although this card was asked for first, it was the last card to be selected; therefore it is sitting on top of the deck.

The key to this demonstration being successful is moving the nine to the top of the flipped pile without being seen. There is a simple way to do this. Pick up the pile with two hands. With your right hand, grab the top card and with your left hand take hold of the rest of the pile. Now you need to flip over the cards to reveal the piles. When flipping, flip both hands at once, but move your right hand above your left as you flip. Now what was the top face-down card becomes the top face-up card and the rest of the cards are in order. You can now dazzle the audience as the cards are revealed in the proper order.

Tips & Techniques

- The theory behind this innovative demonstration is this: With only 13 cards from which to choose, sooner or later an audience member will indeed select the nine of hearts. In fact, each time a spectator chooses a different card, it narrows the field and makes the chances even greater that the next card selected will be the nine.
- Once the nine is selected, you will no longer be one up on the audience, so the demonstration must end immediately. What if the spectator coincidentally selects the nine right off the bat? No problem! Just end the demonstration right there and make it appear as if you and the spectator have a strong mental connection.
- Conversely, it is entirely possible that the nine will not be selected until the last or second to last card. The demonstration will still be just as effective. Remember, when you reveal the cards—as long as you are able to move the nine—it doesn't matter how many cards were drawn. They will still be revealed in the same order in which they were selected. When there are just a few cards left, make believe you don't know what cards are left before saying what to pick. Pretend that you have to consult the list of cards that have been picked to see what's left.

    This variation of the One-Up Principle is very effective because it does indeed eliminate the problem of having the mind reader select one of the cards.

7

Dot's Amazing!

DIFFICULTY LEVEL: ✦✦✦✦✦
IMPACT: ✳✳✳✳✳
PARTNER: YES
PREPARATION: MINIMAL

Overview

This demonstration is so old it was probably first performed by Neanderthal man at cocktail parties in the Stone Age. It is an astonishing feat of mentalism that never fails to shock audiences.

The Premise

While the mind reader is out of the room, her partner hands out envelopes to several spectators. These audience members are asked to place a personal item in an envelope and seal it. When all of the envelopes have been filled and sealed, they are collected by the partner and placed in a large bowl.

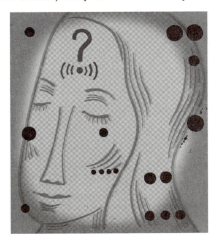

At this point, the mind reader reenters the room and takes her place in front of the audience. She then picks up an envelope, opens it, and removes its contents. After studying the object, she announces to whom the object belongs.

This process is repeated until all of the objects have been correctly identified.

The Solution

The reason that you will be able to identify the owner of the objects is because each envelope will be coded. Of course any type of code will do nicely, but I prefer using minuscule pencil markings placed inconspicuously on the envelopes.

For example, each envelope will have a small dot written on the following areas:

First envelope:	Front upper left corner.
Second envelope:	Front upper right corner.
Third envelope:	Front center.
Fourth envelope:	Front bottom left.
Fifth envelope:	Front bottom right.
Sixth envelope:	Back upper left.
Seventh envelope:	Back upper right.
Eighth envelope:	Back center.
Ninth envelope:	Back lower left.
Tenth envelope:	Back lower right.

You can use more or fewer than ten, depending upon your mood, the situation, and how many people are in the audience. Simply adjust the number of envelopes and their accompanying codes accordingly.

By knowing which audience member had which envelope, you will be able to correctly identify the owner of each object. Whether you decide to use a small or large amount of spectators in this demonstration, you must have a system whereby you can easily remember who was handed each envelope.

Tips & Techniques

- The most important thing to remember is the order in which the envelopes were distributed. Make sure you follow the above system so you will always know the sequence your partner used.
- Now that you know in what order the envelopes were distributed, all you have to do is determine to whom the envelopes were handed. The easiest way to accomplish this would be to have your partner distribute the envelopes in a

systematic fashion. Prior to beginning this demonstration, design a system with your partner.

If there are only five people in your audience, have your partner simply distribute the envelopes to each person in order from left to right. If the spectators are not assembled in any clear order, your partner can manipulate their seating arrangements under the guise that the audience will be able to see the demonstration better.

If there are more audience members than participants, use an easy system to identify the participants. For example, every second person will receive an envelope. If the crowd is not sitting in an orderly fashion and there is not an easy way to rearrange them, limit the number of envelopes to simplify the demonstration.

- Be sure to show some common sense and be very discreet with your markings on the envelope. The last thing you want to do is scribble thick, noticeable marks. If anyone identifies markings on the envelopes, the demonstration will be completely ruined. You might as well just write "Give this envelope to Uncle Seymour" in thick black magic marker across the front of the envelope.

- Every once in a while, you will find a few troublemakers in the audience. These are people who try to interfere with the performance of the demonstration, putting up obstacles every step of the way. In "Dot's Amazing," you might come across the occasional hooligan who tries to switch his envelope with someone else's. Your partner must safeguard against this happening. One way to make sure that the envelopes remain in proper sequence is to hand them out one at a time. When the spectator has placed a personal item in an envelope, your partner can take it back and then hand out the next envelope, so only one spectator is filling an envelope at a time. This, however, is generally not necessary, as the audience will most likely behave.

- When I perform this demonstration in front of friends and family members, I like to entertain the audience (and myself) by poking fun at the participants. Since I already have identified to whom the envelope belongs, I can begin making "predictions" immediately.

When I remove the object, I feel it. I listen to it. And, of course, I smell it thoroughly. I explain that many times the scent of the owner is on the object and that I can often draw an association through odor. The vision then comes to me:

"I am seeing an image of a man ... a rather rotund man ... a man who doesn't like to part with money easily ... [inhaling the scent of the object deeply] ... yes, this object belongs to a frugal man, who some might even call a cheapskate ... a man who would sooner be buried with his fortune than see one penny of it given to his greedy relatives ... in fact, I am surprised he even allowed one of his possessions to be taken from him to be used for this demonstration. Yes, ladies and gentlemen, there is no doubt in my mind that this object belongs to Fred!"

- Obviously, if you do not know the audience, you can tone it down a notch. On several occasions, I have been hired to enact mind reading demonstrations for private social functions. "Dot's Amazing" is one of my favorite to perform because I try to obtain information about some of the partygoers prior to the demonstration.

I enlist the help of the host or the person arranging the event to provide me information regarding the attendees. I then make sure that my partner hands the envelopes to the appropriate people. The impact is staggering when I begin to mention characteristics of complete strangers! Even if the audience suspects that someone fed me information, they are still perplexed how I knew which object belonged to whom.

- Another fun way to reveal the owner of an object is to do so before you even look inside the envelope. You can pretend that the signal you are receiving is so strong that you do not even have to see the object. Simply hand the envelope to the correct person and have him remove the contents to see if you are right.

The Name Game

8

DIFFICULTY LEVEL: ✦✦✦✦
IMPACT: ✳✳✳✳✳
PARTNER: YES
PREPARATION: EXTENSIVE REHEARSAL

Overview

"The Name Game" is a remarkable display of mind reading that never fails to leave audiences bewildered. Once you get a reputation for reading minds, this demonstration is invariably the one that people will call on you to perform—over and over again. Although this exhibition requires considerable practice with a partner, the payoff makes it quite worthwhile. "The Name Game" not only works well in front of a small crowd of three or four people, but also is astonishingly effective for larger audiences of 10 to 50 people.

The first time you perform this demonstration, your partner can announce to the crowd that you have an extraordinary ability to read minds. Yes, there will be skeptics, but you will have an eager audience instantly.

The Premise

The mind reader leaves the room while an audience member is prompted by the partner to state the name of someone famous. When the mind reader returns, he concentrates on the subject who selected the name until he "senses" the secret name. The mind reader then announces the name to a spellbound audience. Works every time!

37

The Solution

Your partner gives you enthusiastic support as you attempt to guess the secret name. What appears to be simple encouragement from your partner is actually a set of cryptic clues to help you discover the answer.

As an example, let's use a name that is selected quite often, Abraham Lincoln. When you return to the room, your partner will proceed to motivate you to reach the answer. After setting the mood with some entertaining showmanship, your partner spells out the answer by uttering carefully concealed hints. *The first letter of each phrase spells out the secret name.* For Abraham Lincoln your partner might say:

"**L**et him concentrate."
"**I**s it coming to you?"
"**N**ow you're getting it."
"**C**ome on already!"
"**O**kay, he's about to get it!"
"**L**et's hear it!"
"**N**ow you have it!"

As you can see, the first letter in each phrase spells out the mystery name.

But won't the audience be able to figure out that the partner is spelling the answer? No! To ensure that the crowd will not guess the secret to this demonstration, there are several tricks you can use to distract the audience (see "Tips & Techniques" for further explanation).

Also, the chances are great that you will have guessed that the answer was Abraham Lincoln long before the partner finished "spelling" the entire clue. When performed properly, it is extremely rare that an audience member will solve the demonstration, even if it is witnessed several times. In addition, there are variations to "The Name Game" that you will learn in this chapter to keep your audience off-balance.

Preparation

The most important aspect for the implementation of this demonstration is making it look natural. This can be accomplished by

being prepared for every letter. The phrases must not appear ⌐
rehearsed clues. Your partner can be creative and direct her
comments to the audience, the subject, or to you, depending on
the clue.

When preparing for this exhibition, you and your partner should
memorize and practice at least two or three clues for each letter.
The reason that you will need several clues is because there may
be two or more of the same letter in a name. Even more likely is
that you will be asked to perform "The Name Game" again and
again—and invariably many letters will be repeated.

There are myriad phrases that can be used for each letter. Of
course, the specific phrases that are used will depend solely on the
personality of the partner giving the clues. The following is a list to
help get you started:

A: Are you concentrating?
    All right everyone, quiet down.
    Any signals yet?

B: Bet you're getting it now.
    Be quiet everyone.
    Believe in yourself.

C: Concentrate!
    Come on!
    Can you get it?

D: Don't rush.
Do you have it?
Don't make him nervous.

E: Everyone concentrate.
Enough talking.
Easy does it.

F: Free your mind.
Feel anything yet?
Fascinate us.

G: Getting anything?
Give us the answer.
Got it?

H: He's really concentrating now.
Hurry!
He might need some help concentrating.

I: I know he's getting close.
Is it coming to you?
It's a hard one.

J: Just tell us.
Jeepers!
Just say it already!

K: Know it?
Keep concentrating.
Keep it up.

L: Let us hear it!
Let's all concentrate.
Let's go.

M: Make it a good one.
Must you take so long?
Man oh man, this is a hard one.

N: Now you have it.
Nobody say anything.
No, don't let it slip away!

O: Oh boy! He has it!
Okay, he's about to get it.
Oh no, are you getting it?

P: Please tell us!
Patience, please.
Pick the right one.

Q: Quickly.
Quiet everyone.
Quite difficult.

R: Relax.
Read his/her mind.
Ready?

S: Say it.
Silence!
Shhh!

T: Take your time.
Tell us!
Today, please!

U: Unbelievable.
Up to you now.
Unleash your powers.

V: Very quiet now.
Victory is near!
Very nice.

W: We all have to concentrate.
We've got it.
We don't have all day.

X: (See *Tips & Techniques* below.)

Y: You've got it!
       You're not concentrating.
       Yes, feel the vibes.

Z: (See *Tips & Techniques* below.)

The success of this demonstration rests solely on the communication between the partner and the mind reader. Practice and creativity will enhance the impact of this spectacular exhibition.

If you stop reading these instructions now, you already have enough information to perform this demonstration successfully most of the time. To add to the impact and excitement of "The Name Game" and to ensure that the demonstration is executed flawlessly, here are a few hints and special instructions:

Tips & Techniques

- Since there are no simple clues for "X" or "Z" there is an easy method you can use to get around this problem. You and your partner can decide on particular phrases that will always mean "X" or "Z." For example, "This is a hard one" can mean "X," and "This is an easy one" can mean "Z."
- When you are out of the room and your partner hears the secret name, she must decide whether to give clues for the first or last name. This decision should be based upon which name would be easier to communicate and receive.

    If a subject suggests the name George Washington, the last name would be a better choice, since there is no certainty that you will guess "George Washington" just from deciphering "George." After all, the subject could have said George Burns, George Bush, or George Foreman. By guessing "Washington," you can be reasonably sure that the answer is George Washington.
- To make it easier, your partner should let you know if she is spelling the first name or last name as soon as you return to the room. This can be accomplished with a simple phrase such as, "You're going to get this one" for the first name, or

"You'll never get this one" to indicate the last name. When one-name celebrities are mentioned, such as Cher or Madonna, this step can be ignored.

- It is helpful to "pad" the clues with other phrases before the real clues begin so that the audience will never catch on to your system. One of these phrases can be what was discussed in the previous tip, "You're going to get this one." You and your partner can work out a system that will indicate when the real clues will begin.

- Once this demonstration is performed a number of times in front of the same audience, the likelihood of the code being discovered increases. To minimize this possibility, it is best to change the delivery system slightly. This can get a little complicated, but is very effective for keeping the audience off track.

    For example, when the partner uses an "A" phrase, she is really indicating the letter "B," and so on. So "Are you ready" is actually a clue for "B" and not "A." This will throw off any observer who may be close to deciphering the answer to "The Name Game."

    Also, at any point during the demonstration, if you or your partner sense that an audience member may be catching on, he or she can say "I'm way ahead of you," indicating that from now on, the clues will be a letter ahead. This is an advanced technique and requires much practice before using it.

- After you have performed this demonstration a number of times, you may notice that certain names are repeated over and over. If this is the case, you and your partner may want to develop a special set of shortcuts for the most common names. This will save time and minimize the amount of clues that needs to be exchanged.

- To make this demonstration even more fun to witness, you and your partner can be quite entertaining by bantering back and forth with each other while the clues are being given. In the example where the secret name is Abraham Lincoln, a dialogue could transpire as follows:

Partner: Let him concentrate.

Mind Reader: Yes, please let me concentrate.

Partner:	Is it coming to you?
Mind Reader:	Well, it would if you'd keep quiet and let me concentrate.
Partner:	Now you're getting it.
Mind Reader:	I'm getting what? I'm getting a headache. Who could concentrate with your constant yapping?
Partner:	C'mon already!

And so forth. As long as you can keep your concentration on the clues, the bantering can continue throughout the demonstration.

In any event, you should practice enough so that you feel comfortable enough to talk back and forth with your partner. This will make the demonstration appear more natural, and will distract the audience from the fact that clues are being given.

- It should be noted that most observers will know that there is some type of clue system being used, but it is very difficult to figure out the secret.

- During the exhibition, you will, at some point, figure out what the secret name is. Most likely, this realization will occur far before your partner has finished giving the clues. An experienced mind reader will be able to guess Abraham Lincoln by the third letter—perhaps even the second letter if he is willing to take a chance.

- When you finally figure out the secret name, you should not immediately blurt out the answer. Oh, no—first have some fun with it. You might even want to start a dialogue with the subject, saying something like:

"I am beginning to get a sense of something. I am starting to see a number. That's strange. Why on earth would I see a number? I am trying to think of a name. Oh, here it is. It's the number 16. 16. That is strange. Now I am beginning to see money. Hmm, let's see. It's becoming clearer now. It's a dollar bill! Oh, wait. I'm wrong. It's not a dollar bill. It's a five-dollar bill! Yes, the image is getting clearer. A five-dollar bill! And whose face do you think is staring at me from that five-dollar bill? Why, it is none other than the 16th president of the United States, Abraham Lincoln!"

- A great variation of this demonstration adds a new dimension to the clue-giving process. In this version, when your partner is giving clues, the vowels are substituted with hand clapping or snapping sounds. For example:

    A = one clap
    E = two claps
    I = three claps
    O = four claps
    U = five claps

  In the Abraham Lincoln example, your partner would clap twice for the "I" and not use a phrase. When your partner reaches the "O," four claps would be used.

  The claps can be done right in front of your face as if it is an attempt to awaken a mind reading spirit, or perhaps to make sure that you are alert.

  Whatever version you decide to use, "The Name Game" promises to be a fun and astonishing demonstration. But be careful; once you perform "The Name Game," it will be expected from you at every social event thereafter!

- One final variation is to have your partner spell out a clue for the person, rather than the name. For Abraham Lincoln, your partner might give you clues that lead to "PENNY PREZ." You can then figure out that that means Lincoln. All of the above methods can be used in any combination with this method. This variation is particularly hard for the audience to pick up on.

Cheating

Looking for a shortcut? There is a way that you can eliminate the need to exchange signals with your partner. This method is risky and not recommended if there is even the slightest chance of being discovered. I only mention this technique because there are times when it will come in handy.

At large parties or gatherings, there is usually a lot of commotion, and distractions abound. In these situations, I found it helpful to enlist the help of a second partner. While I am out of the room, my first partner introduces the demonstration and has the audience decide on a name that I will have to guess. While this is happening, my second partner is standing near the group of people, just listening, pretending to be a part of another conversation entirely.

When the name is selected, I am called back into the room. Here is where the cheating comes in:

As I am reentering the room, my second partner walks past me and casually whispers the secret name. I do not acknowledge this partner, nor do I confirm that I heard the name. I simply keep walking to the crowd of people as if I am about to perform the demonstration.

If, for some reason, I was unable to hear the name, I continue with the demonstration as originally planned. But, if my second partner successfully revealed the secret name to me, then I can dispense with the exchanging of clues and get right to the climax of the demonstration. When this is done effectively, the impact is tremendous. The audience is stunned that I am able to guess the secret name *without a single clue being given!*

By the way, don't be afraid to have your partner sneak you clues surreptitiously. If all eyes are on you, and your partner can "mouth" the answer to you with no one seeing, you should take advantage of it. Remember, playing the part of a mind reader is all about being sneaky in the first place, so feel free to cheat any way you can.

Sleight of Mind

DIFFICULTY LEVEL: ✦✦✦✦✦
IMPACT: ✹✹✹✹✹
PARTNER: YES
PREPARATION: NONE

Overview

This interesting and bizarre demonstration is great fun for both the mind reader and the audience. Although the execution of this feat is simple to perform, it is often difficult for the audience to decipher. The best part of this demonstration is that it provides an opportunity to add humor in a disturbing, almost frightening way. Intrigued? Read on.

The Premise

At first, this fun demonstration appears to be nothing more than a simple card trick. The mind reader leaves the room while his partner openly shuffles a borrowed deck of cards. A spectator is asked to select a card and show it to the audience. Once all of the onlookers have had a chance to view the card, it is placed randomly back into the deck.

The entire deck of cards is then given to another spectator. She is asked to hand-deliver the deck to the mind reader in the other room. Over the next several minutes, strange noises are heard from the mind reader's room. At some point the mind reader reappears into the main room and announces the correct card to the audience.

The Solution

As described above, the demonstration appears to be a simple card trick. You announce that you will leave the room while an audience member selects a card. Upon your return you will correctly name the card.

Once the audience is satisfied that you are in another room and cannot possibly see or hear what is happening, your partner borrows or produces a deck, removes the cards from the case, and shuffles them thoroughly. Of course, the audience is free to inspect the deck to their satisfaction. Convinced that it is a clean deck, your partner fans out the cards and asks a spectator to choose one.

For verification, everyone in the room is allowed to see what was selected. Your partner should *not* be allowed to see the card, though. Otherwise, the audience will suspect that your partner somehow signaled to you what the card was. While the audience inspects the card, your partner places the deck back into its case— but upside down. *The cards must be put back into the case facing up.* Once the audience is finished looking at the chosen card, the spectator is asked to replace the card back into the deck, which is in the case.

The spectator naturally places the card into the hidden deck face down, assuming that all of the cards are facing down. In reality, only the selected card is facing down, while the others are facing up. This will make it ridiculously simple for you to discover the secret card.

Once the card is replaced, the case is sealed and given to another spectator to deliver to you in the next room.

Tips & Techniques

There is a teensy-weensy problem with this demonstration. Unless your audience is distracted, it is quite possible that someone in the audience will realize that the deck is upside down. To minimize this possibility, encourage your partner to hasten the presentation as much as possible. I find that when the pace is fast and the spectators feel a sense of urgency, they are less likely to notice the details as much.

Another way to guard against the audience discovering that the deck is upside down is to secretly flip the bottom card over so that both end cards have their backs showing. If you use this technique, you can even pull the deck forward so that the cards are protruding from the pack. If the audience sees that the top card is facing down, they will assume that the entire deck is facing down.

Let's face it: Once the deck is delivered to you in the next room, it will take no time at all for you to discover the secret card. You simply remove the deck from the case and look for the only card that is facing the opposite direction from the others.

Of course, you could easily walk into the next room and simply state the card. A simple, no-frills demonstration.

Ho hum. Yawn.

It is difficult to imagine that your audience would be anything but unimpressed and left with a damp, hungry feeling. The hunger to which I refer is an empty starvation for entertainment. Don't do this to your audience. They don't deserve it. Instead you have an opportunity to demonstrate to the spectators how truly weird you really are. Up for it?

If so, you must first adopt an attitude whereby it seems as if you do not want to perform this demonstration. Perhaps your partner can suggest that you perform "Sleight of Mind" and you outright refuse. Have your partner keep prodding you along, asking you to perform this particular demonstration.

You still refuse, claiming that it is far too difficult to perform, but most of all it's just too painful. You are not mentally prepared to go through that agony just for the sake of impressing everyone in the room. You can explain, however, that you would be happy to perform any number of other spectacular feats of telepathy, but—although you are deeply sorry— "Sleight of Mind" is out of the question.

Hopefully at this point, the audience will have joined in with your partner in asking you to perform this demonstration. After a few more minutes of refusing, you can finally relent and agree to perform this earth-shattering, but extremely painful demonstration.

You should be stating this in an overexaggerated manner so that the audience will realize that you are only pretending to be against the performance. As you leave to wait in the

49

other room, you could mumble something like, "Oh why must I suffer so for my talent? Why oh why was I blessed with this superhuman gift?"

After a few moments, a spectator will knock on your door to hand you the sealed deck. The audience will be waiting quietly in the next room, awaiting your return to reveal the secret card. For the first minute or so, there should be complete silence.

The audience will certainly wonder what on earth are you doing in there with the cards. After a minute of silence, the audience will then hear gentle weeping coming from your room. This barely audible crying begins to get louder with each passing second, until it becomes uncontrollable, mock wailing.

If someone from the audience should suggest looking in on you to see what is going on, your partner should take charge and block the way into the room, saying, "Please, just let him be. You cruel people are the ones who insisted that he perform this demonstration. Now you will have to sit here and listen to his agony. Can you appreciate how much this brave, compassionate man suffers for your entertainment?"

After another moment or so, your wails can turn into pleading and begging. Let the audience hear unintelligible mumblings from you, as if you are beseeching some Supreme Being to provide assistance in identifying this card.

Perhaps some clanging around will help your cause. Sounds of objects falling and banging into each other should mix in with your pleading and sobbing. If you have time to prepare, you can play a cassette tape of utter chaos. The audience will hear glass breaking, people screaming, cows mooing, a baby crying, police sirens, a bomb explosion— whatever you can conjure to add to the imbroglio. When you have sufficiently made your point, the sounds can slowly abate. If you really want to ham it up, once the noises have quieted, you can start them up again.

When you feel that you have sucked every last drop of humor out of this routine, it is time to proceed to the conclusion.

Finally, the noises dissipate. The door to your room is pushed open. You take two steps and enter the performing area. You are completely dazed, your clothing disheveled, your hair all askew. With a little preparation you can add special effects. Perhaps a cloud of smoke emerges from the room

with you (from the bomb explosion), or fake blood is on your face, or your shirt is on backwards, etc.

You are breathing heavily and have trouble standing. As if you are on the brink of passing out, you walk to the middle of the room, reach your hand in your pocket and produce a card. As you are about to hold it up to the audience, you collapse to the ground, landing on your back with your hand sticking straight out, the selected card in full view of the audience.

If you are up for it, your partner can splash a bit of water in your face to revive you amidst a sea of awe and applause from the audience.

10

364

DIFFICULTY LEVEL: ✦✦✦✦✦
IMPACT: ✹✹✹✹✹
PARTNER: NO
PREPARATION: EXTENSIVE PRACTICE

Overview

As you can see, this next demonstration has a difficulty rating of 5 with an impact of only 2. Is it worth all of the practice for such a mediocre payoff? You will have to decide that for yourself.

There are some mind reading demonstrations that make the performer appear is if he has a razor-sharp mind with almost superhuman memory. "364" just happens to be one of those feats. This is a complex demonstration that requires more thought than any other in this book. You will find that by using a little brainpower and a lot of concentration, you can master this impressive system.

The Premise

The mind reader's claim in this demonstration is that he has a photographic memory. The host of the party produces a deck of cards, which is shuffled thoroughly by a spectator. When the audience is satisfied that the deck is completely mixed, another spectator is asked to remove a card. This card is shown to the other people in the room for verification.

Contrary to most card "tricks," the selected card is *not* replaced in the deck. It is kept aside by a spectator for safekeeping.

The mind reader then asks another spectator to show him the remaining cards, one at a time. When the deck has been shown to the mind reader in its entirety, he announces the missing card.

Pretty good, huh?

The Solution

After a spectator has selected a card and shown it to the audience, another spectator will show you the remaining cards. It is important that you instruct this spectator to reveal the cards one at a time. As each card is presented, you are quietly counting. When the entire deck has been shown to you, you will—secretly—have a sum of all of the remaining cards.

The answer to this puzzle is incredibly simple, but it requires intense concentration and strong math skills. The name of this demonstration is "364," which not coincidentally, is the sum of all of the cards added together. Yes, if you count up all of the cards, the total amount will be 364. The method of counting is as follows:

Ace:	1
Two through ten:	Face value
Jack:	11
Queen:	12
King:	13

Have you figured it out yet?

When one of the cards is removed from the deck, the total amount of the cards remaining will no longer be 364. To determine the number of the secret card, you must first calculate the sum of the remaining cards. For the sake of this explanation, let's assume that the card selected was a seven of clubs. This will mean that the total sum of the remaining cards will be 357. Well, it only takes some basic subtraction to figure out that the missing card is a seven.

What's the matter? Does it seem too difficult for you? Afraid of adding a few numbers? Oh, dear reader, show some character! As the cards are revealed to you, all you have to do is add them up. It's only math. It won't kill you.

I believe that I know you well enough by now to realize that you have a question. You're wondering how you're going to miraculously figure out the suit.

Well, you're not going to like this, but there is no easy way. I am about to explain to you how you can identify the suit, but it will require even more effort on your part. Don't panic; just keep an open mind.

When you are counting the cards in your head, be on the look-out for two suits. I like to pick spades and hearts. Why? No particular reason. If you are partial to clubs and diamonds I would have no problem with it (although it should be one red suit and one black suit).

Use your fingers on your left hand to keep count of spades. Each time another spade appears, secretly put up one finger. When you have reached five, start all over. After the deck is through, you will have either two or three fingers showing. Obviously, if only two fingers are showing, that will mean that only 12 spades have been counted, and the card selected was indeed a spade. Conversely, if you have three fingers up, you can eliminate spades from consideration, because all of the 13 spades have been accounted for.

One of the great things about being human is that we were blessed with the use of two hands. While your left hand is counting spades, you will use your right hand to count hearts. As before, you will secretly put up a finger each time a heart is revealed. By using this method, you will be able to determine whether the card is a spade or a heart.

I am not going to ask you to count the other two suits on your toes. That would be ridiculous. Instead, use your eyebrows. (Just kidding, relax!)

If you have determined that the card is a spade or a heart, you will be able to correctly identify the missing card. If you have determined that the card is not a spade or a heart, then you are left with a 50-50 possibility. If this unfortunate predicament occurs, you have two options.

Option #1: You know it is either a club or diamond. Take a guess.

Option #2: Ask the audience if the card is red or black. Since you have narrowed the choices down to one red suit and one black suit, knowing the color of the missing card will eliminate any guesswork.

Tips & Techniques

What makes this demonstration so effective is that the audience will generally not suspect that you have so much time on your hands that you sat down and figured out the sum of all of the cards and then proceeded to add them up in front of them. Ah, how little they know you.

As mentioned before, the only way to perfect this demonstration is through intense concentration. And this can only be achieved through practice. I realize how impossible it appears to try adding numbers while you are keeping track of two different suits. If you put the time into practicing, you will find that is not as difficult as you think.

In Las Vegas, Atlantic City, and other venues where gambling is legal, there are numerous blackjack players who attempt to gain an advantage on the house by "counting cards." This technique is similar to the one employed in "364" in the respect that it uses a mathematical counting system to make a determination.

If, by using the finger counting method, you have been unable to determine the exact suit, it would be a good idea to prepare the audience for the possibility that you may not get it 100% correct by mentioning that you have a clear picture in your mind of the number, but are having a difficult time identifying the suit.

If you are planning to take a 50-50 chance and guess at the suit, indicate to the audience that you are trying to narrow it down. After the cards have been shown to you, you can place your hand on your temples, close your eyes, and say something along the lines of:

"I'm just sorting through the cards in my mind ... I can see that it is definitely not a picture card ... definitely not an ace ... I am seeing something in the middle of the deck ... Let's see ... is it a seven, eight, or nine ... okay, it's not an eight, and

I am willing to bet the farm that it's not a nine. Why would it be a nine? Oh, wait a minute; maybe it is a nine ... No, I was right. I remember seeing all four nines ... so, according to my reasoning, that means it must be a seven ... Wait! ... Yes, it is definitely a seven!"

This should be impressive enough. After all, you just accurately selected the number of the card that was selected from the deck. A one in thirteen chance! Of course, you know audiences; they are never satisfied until you pick the suit. You can continue:

"Now for the suit ... I am trying to remember seeing all of the suits ... Wow, it's such a blur ... Okay, I am starting to narrow it down. I remember seeing so many spades ... ten, jack, queen, king, ace ... yes, all of the spades are there. It is definitely *not* a spade ... I am counting the hearts, I believe they are all there ... yes, if I am not mistaken ... ten, jack, queen, king, ace ... yes, I remember seeing all of the hearts ... Okay, it is definitely *not* a heart ... That just leaves clubs and diamonds ... was it a club or diamond ... it's getting so hazy ... club or diamond ..."

Whatever you select, say it with confidence. Open your eyes, look directly at the audience and say, *"The card is a seven of clubs!"*

The odds are in your favor in this demonstration. You see, you have two 50-50 chances of getting the suit correct. The first chance is when you use your fingers to count. According to the odds, the card will be a spade or heart *half* of the time. In the event that it is a club or a diamond, then you have another 50-50 chance of getting it right.

I am sure you realize that even though the odds are in your favor, there is still a chance that you can get the suit wrong. But will that be so terrible? After all, you correctly identified the number of the card, and you had narrowed the suits down to just club or diamond. The audience will still be very impressed.

If you are bothered by the thought that you may get the suit wrong, then simply use Plan B. Ask the audience if it is a red or black card. If it is red, obviously it is a diamond; and if it is black, the suit is a club.

Another Method

I am going to present to you a complex way of knowing *for sure* what suit was selected. I warn you: It is not for the weak-hearted.

On one of your hands, you will keep track of the suits as follows: Each time a spade is introduced, do nothing. When you see a heart, put up an additional finger. For diamonds, put up two more fingers. And for clubs, add three fingers to what you already have up. If you need to put up five or more fingers, subtract five from the number and put that number up. So if you have four fingers up and a club comes next, you'd add three fingers to four to get seven, which is the same as two, since you always subtract five if you're above four.

At the end of the deck, if you have three fingers up, the missing card is a spade. If two fingers are left up, the mystery card is a heart. If you have one finger up, it's a diamond. If you're left with no fingers standing, then the card is a club. In the unlikely event that you have four fingers up, you've made a mistake somewhere along the way or you're not playing with a full deck.

Let me explain. If all 52 cards were exposed, there would be 13 cards in each suit. The spades would make no fingers go up, the hearts would make 13 go up, the diamonds 26, and the clubs 39. That adds up to 78 fingers up. But since you roll over and subtract five whenever you get above four, 78 is the same as 3, since if you keep subtracting 5 from 78, you eventually get to 3. So if you have two fingers up at the end, the last card must be a heart to make you end with three fingers up. Similar logic rules for the other totals. This may sound confusing to you, but my advice is not to worry about it. Just accept that it is a mathematical fact. Try it. You will see that it works!

To sum up, use the chart:

Fingers Up at the End	Missing Card
No fingers up	Club
One finger up	Diamond
Two fingers up	Heart
Three fingers up	Spade

I am sure that this method of counting will be quite elementary for someone with such an agile, advanced mind, such as you.

It takes a bit of practice, but after a while, it comes naturally that you're working in base 5 so $4 + 3 = 2$.

Since you're doing this at the same time as adding up the value of the cards, things can get confusing. It's important to set an order for the process and stick to it. Always add the value of the card first, and then do the suit. Otherwise you'll forget whether you've done one of the additions already. And remember: Practice makes perfect.

11

It All Adds Up

DIFFICULTY LEVEL: ✦✦✦✦✦
IMPACT: ✹✹✹✹✹
PARTNER: NO
PREPARATION: REQUIRED PLANNING/SETUP

Overview

Sometimes I think that I should stop performing this next demonstration, because it is quite possible that it may actually cause damage to someone one day. When people see this miracle performed, they are stunned to such a high degree, they tend to become disoriented and profoundly bewildered. Have you ever been profoundly bewildered? It isn't pleasant. This feat is so stunning, that I am afraid it could inflict brain hemorrhaging to those who witness it. I will explain to you how to master this demonstration, but please, if you insist on performing it, exercise extreme caution.

The reason that this demonstration is so mind-boggling is because the mentalist appears to predict a randomly selected word before the demonstration begins! This is a mind reading feat on a larger scale than the others described in this book, and requires six volunteers.

The Premise

The mind reader announces to the audience that she has developed a psychic technique that allows her to predict events in the future. To prove it, she has developed a demonstration for the audience.

Step #1: The mind reader selects a spectator from the audience, and hands him a dictionary. The spectator is then asked to return to his seat in the audience.

59

Step #2: A second subject from the audience is selected, and handed a sealed envelope. This subject is also asked to take his seat back in the audience.

Hello? Are you with me? Pay attention! So far, one audience member has a dictionary and another audience member has a sealed envelope. It gets a little more complicated here, so read carefully.

Step #3: An audience member is asked to approach the performing area and write a three-digit number on a piece of paper. This audience member then returns to her seat.

Another audience member is asked to approach the performing area and write another three-digit number on the same piece of paper, directly under the first number.

Finally, one more audience member is asked to do the same: Write down a three-digit number on the same piece of paper, directly below the other two.

So, now on the piece of paper is a list of three three-digit numbers. It will look something like this:

1. 341
2. 638
3. 834

Step #4: Another audience member is asked to approach the performing area and tally the three three-digit numbers. Yes, you can hand the volunteer a calculator.

What you are about to read may not seem possible, but just wait until I show you how to do it!

Step #5: The audience member who added the numbers announces the total. For the sake of this explanation, let's just say that number is 1813.

The mind reader then calls the very first audience member back to the performing area. For those of you who have been paying attention, you will know that I am referring to the spectator with the dictionary.

The mind reader announces that the number that was calculated, 1813, is going to be used to locate a specific word in the dictionary. She further explains that the first three digits of the number (181) will be used to identify the page in the dictionary. The last digit will indicate how many boldfaced entries down.

Since the last digit is a 3, that means that the third boldfaced entry on page 181 of the dictionary is the selected word.

After explaining this, the spectator holding the dictionary is asked to turn to the selected page number (181) and count down three boldfaced entries. For the sake of this explanation, let's assume that the word is "Perception."

Do you see where this is going?

Once the secret word has been revealed, the mind reader asks the spectator with the sealed envelope to approach the performing area. With great drama and anticipation, the spectator is asked to unseal the envelope and pull out its contents.

The spectator then opens the envelope, reaches in and pulls out a slip of paper. The mind reader then asks this spectator to read what is written on the piece of paper to the audience.

And what do you think that the word is? Yes! "Perception!"

Isn't that mind boggling??? Come on now, admit it: If you could pull that off and have the word in the envelope match the word that was identified in the dictionary, would this be the most miraculous demonstration ever conceived? The good news is that you can! And this is how:

The Solution

The beginning of this demonstration is very straightforward. As described above, two audience members are asked to hold onto a dictionary and a sealed envelope.

Also, as described above, three more spectators are chosen to write down three three-digit numbers on a piece of paper. Here is the crucial part:

Once the three numbers have been written on the paper, and the audience members return to their seats, you then lift up the paper and announce that there are three three-digit numbers on the sheet of paper, and you need someone from the audience—who is good at math—to approach the performing area and add the three numbers.

The spectator who is chosen then approaches the performing area and sits down at a table. At this point, you place the sheet of paper on the table—but *turned over!*

The spectator, instead of seeing the three numbers that the audience members had written down, now sees a different set of numbers—written beforehand by you!

And will this spectator have any clue that the numbers he sees are not authentic? Of course not! After all, he doesn't know which numbers were selected by the audience, and it is highly unlikely that he will recognize the handwriting of any of the participants.

So let's now play out the rest of the demonstration.

The spectator adds the numbers, announces the total (1813), and takes his seat back in the audience. The word in the dictionary matches the word in the envelope, the audience breaks out into wild applause, and you are carried out of the room on their bewildered shoulders.

Exciting, huh?

Preparation

Unlike many demonstrations in this book, this particular feat does require some simple preparation. First, you must locate a page in the dictionary and select a secret word.

The page you select must fall between 100 and 299. It is suggested that you choose a page somewhere in the middle. Then select a word that is not more than nine boldfaced entries down. Obviously, this is because the most the last digit could possibly be is nine.

Once you have selected a word, write it on a piece of plain white paper using a thick black magic marker. Writing it in bold, dark letters on a stark white piece of paper seems to add to the impact and intensity of the payoff of this demonstration.

Then fold the paper in half, and then in quarters. Place the paper into a standard business-sized envelope and seal it. If you prefer, you can place this envelope into a larger envelope and seal it. For a longer build-up, you can even place these envelopes inside one or two larger envelopes.

You must also prepare the sheet of paper with the three three-digit numbers. As per our example above, if the page number is 181 and the word you have selected is the third entry down, your sum will be 1813. By using simple addition and subtraction, find three three-digit numbers that add up to 1813.

Write the numbers in the upper left-handed corner of the page. It should look something like this:

1. 341
2. 638
3. 834

Once you completed this, flip the paper over, turn it upside down, and write just the numbers 1, 2, and 3, as indicated:

1.
2.
3.

And that is all the preparation you need!

Tips & Techniques

- Are you worried that someone will see you turning the piece of paper over? Well, don't be. It's so simple! This is because, at that point in the demonstration, the audience does not know where it is heading, and they are not on the lookout for any foul play. Also, they are concentrating on the person being selected to tally the numbers. They are not paying attention to the sheet of paper in your hand. The audience is still trying to figure out the significance of the three numbers, and its relation to the dictionary and the sealed envelope. No one will notice as you nonchalantly place the paper down on the table upside down.
- Make sure that you use a pencil and not a pen; it is less likely to show through the paper. It is also important that the stock of paper you select is not too thin. It is recommended that you use a 24-pound paper that is not transparent. This way, when the audience members are writing down their three-digit numbers, they will not notice that there is any writing on the back of the paper.
- When you prepare the sheet of paper, be careful where you write the three-digit numbers and the numbers 1, 2, and 3. Not only should you write these numbers on opposite sides of the paper, you should also write them at opposite ends of

the paper. This is to minimize the chance of a spectator seeing a shadow of numbers on the other side.

- Although this may seem like common sense, it is worth noting that as a precaution you will need to change the handwriting for each of the three-digit numbers. You wouldn't have to be Einstein to suspect something fishy if all three three-digit numbers were written in the same handwriting.
- When asking for a volunteer from the audience to add the numbers, you can keep the demonstration lighthearted through humor. For example: When it is time to add the numbers, you can say that you need a volunteer who is good at math; someone who can add. When a volunteer raises his hand, say, "No, I'm sorry, I said that I need someone who can add, but thanks anyway."
- Get rid of the piece of paper with the numbers on it as soon as possible. Once the numbers have been tallied and the sum read aloud by the audience member, take the paper and discreetly hide it in your pocket. At your very next opportunity, dispose of the sheet of paper completely. Many times a spectator will ask to see the paper when the trick is over.
- If you prefer, you can use a large blackboard to write the answer (1813) once the spectator has calculated it.
- Toward the end of the demonstration when the word from the dictionary has been identified, you can use this opportunity to have some fun with the audience. This is the best possible position in which you can be. The sleight of hand has worked perfectly and the evidence (the sheet of paper) has been removed. Now all that's left is for the spectator to open the envelope and read the secret word to the audience.

Well, you know very well what the word is, and unless there was a mathematical error, the word written on the paper inside the envelope will indeed match the word that has been identified in the dictionary. This is your chance to savor the moment and ham up the ending. After all, it can't hurt to be a little brazen at this point since you know how the demonstration will conclude.

You can say something like:

"Now let's recap everything we have just seen. Before this demonstration began, I wrote a word on a piece of paper and placed it inside an envelope. This sealed envelope was placed inside another envelope and given to a member in the audience. Then three audience members came up, each writing a three-digit number on a piece of paper. I will remind you that they selected their numbers of their own free will with absolutely no coaching from me.

"Those numbers were then added to give us a four-digit sum. We then found the appropriate word on the given page in the dictionary." You can then ask the holder of the dictionary to remind the audience of the secret word. Once this is done, you continue:

"The word is 'perception.' It is now time to take a look inside the envelope to see what was written. First, let me ask you something. If the word 'perception' is written on a piece of paper inside the envelope, would this be the single most impressive feat you have ever witnessed in your lifetime?" (Wait for the response.)

"Seriously, will this be considered forever more by all of you here today to be the most breathtaking, mind-blowing demonstration ever performed?" (Wait for the response.) "Will I be proclaimed by all of you as the smartest, most spectacular human being ever to walk the face of the earth?" (If they try to deny your superhuman status, you can threaten to not reveal the secret word. Once they have satisfied your egomaniacal hunger by agreeing with you, it is finally time to conclude the demonstration.)

"Now that we fully understand each other, let's take a look to see what the secret word is." Then say to the person with the envelope: "Will you please open the envelope and show the audience the secret word?"

You then take deep, well-deserved bows.

A Great Variation

Yes, the dictionary demonstration is truly earth shattering. I agree. But some people are not satisfied with a mere miracle. They need to reach a higher level, a level for which there is no appropriate word. For those people—and you may very well be one of them—I offer the following variation.

Instead of using just one envelope, you will use two. The first envelope contains the secret word. The second envelope contains a person's name and telephone number. These envelopes are handed to two different audience members as in Step #2 described earlier in this demonstration.

Once the dictionary has been given to an audience member, a telephone directory is then produced and given to another audience member.

Instead of having audience members write down three-digit numbers on one piece of paper, you will ask them to each write *two separate three-digit numbers* on two different sheets of paper. This will barely add any time to the length of the demonstration and opens it up to a completely new dimension. After the numbers have been written, two separate volunteers are selected to add the numbers on both sheets. Of course, both pieces of paper are discreetly flipped over to reveal your preselected numbers before the volunteers perform the addition.

Are you following this? If not reread the last paragraph, because it is important!

At the end of the demonstration, the word in the dictionary is identified, and the secret word in the envelope is revealed. But the demonstration is not over! You still have *two* more impossible surprises for the audience.

The first surprise involves the second group of numbers. When this total is revealed, the person with the telephone directory is brought up to the performing area. The same process that was used with the dictionary is followed with the telephone directory. The first three numbers indicate the page number, while the last digit indicates how many names down. When the person holding the telephone directory has identified the name, it is announced to the audience (and, if you prefer, written on a blackboard).

At this time, the person with the second envelope is brought up to the performing area and asked to read what is in the envelope. Of course, the name and telephone number written on the paper is the same one that was just announced from the telephone directory.

That's the first surprise. Here's the second (hold on to your chairs!):

You walk over to the telephone, pick it up, and call the person written on the piece of paper.

Yes, reader, you read it correctly. *You call the person on the telephone!* Am I insane? Possibly. But read on.

You then either use a speakerphone or ask an audience member to get on the telephone. *The person you called is then asked to identify the secret word that was found in the dictionary!!!*

Huh?

Yes! This "randomly chosen stranger" is asked to name the secret word that was written on the paper in the first envelope. And guess what! *She answers correctly!*

Now it's pure bedlam. When the correct answer is revealed, your audience will be in such a state of shock, they very well might get up and run out of the building, screaming into the night for their mommies.

And how does this stranger know what the word is? Well, obviously this person is not a stranger. You rigged the demonstration so that the name chosen from the directory is someone you know. Also, the word has been preselected and revealed to your friend beforehand. Just make sure she is home prior to beginning the demonstration.

And if calling the person on the telephone isn't outlandish enough for you, you can go one step further. Preselect someone you know who lives within walking distance. Escort your audience down the street to the address of the person found in the telephone directory. Simply open the mailbox and remove another envelope. When this envelope is opened, the same secret word is revealed.

If you are unbalanced enough to try this variation, you will have to amend part of this demonstration. Instead of three-digit numbers, you may have to use four-digit numbers. This is because you may have to go deeper into the telephone book to get to a page where you actually know someone.

This variation involves many more steps and much more preparation. Also, the potential for something to go wrong in this version is increased significantly. Is it worth the final mind-blowing payoff? It's up to you to decide.

*My W*ord!

DIFFICULTY LEVEL: ✦✦✦✦✦
IMPACT: ✳✳✳✳✳
PARTNER: NO
PREPARATION: SOME MEMORIZATION AND SETUP

Overview

Okay, so you like the idea of using a dictionary, but you don't like using so many volunteers. I hear you. Let's learn a simple demonstration that uses a dictionary but requires far fewer participants.

The Premise

In this simple but effective demonstration, the mind reader announces that he can visualize every word in the dictionary. This statement will undoubtedly be met with skepticism. The mind reader then announces he will prove it through a simple exercise.

A spectator is handed a pen and a piece of paper and is asked to write down a three-digit number. The only restriction is that none of the digits may repeat. Other than that slight inconvenience, this spectator is free to choose from the literally hundreds of three-digit numbers still remaining.

The volunteer you have selected is then asked to reverse the number. For the sake of this explanation, let's assume that the spectator wrote 345. The reverse of that number is 543.

Finally, the spectator is asked to subtract the smaller number from the larger and write down the result. In our example, the difference between 543 and 345 is 198.

A dictionary is produced and handed to another spectator. Similar to the previous demonstration, "It All Adds Up," we will use the number (in this case 198) to locate a word in the dictionary.

The first two numbers will indicate the page number, while the last number will tell us how many boldfaced words down the page.

This would mean that the spectator should open the dictionary to page 19 and search for the eighth word down. Prior to the word being revealed, the mind reader writes his prediction on a slip of paper and hands it to another spectator.

The volunteer with the dictionary then announces the eighth word down on page 19. The spectator with the slip of paper then opens it and reads the prediction to the audience. Miraculously, the words match.

The Solution

It's really quite simple: Just memorize every single word in the entire dictionary.

Oh, I see, you're not willing to put in the time to do something worthwhile? Okay, okay ... let me make it a lot easier for you. You only have to memorize nine words. Yes, only nine! And here is why:

Mathematically it works out the same no matter what three-digit numbers are selected. When the numbers are reversed, and the smaller number is subtracted from the larger, there are only nine possible answers. And they are:

99, 198, 297, 396, 495, 594, 693, 792, and 891.

Why is this so? It's just one of those mathematical oddities. Use it to your advantage.

So, now that you know that there can only be nine possible answers, all you have to do is memorize the nine words in the dictionary that correspond with each answer. Hey, what's with the face? At least you don't have to memorize every word in the dictionary!

Tips and Techniques

There is another way to present this demonstration that can be quite sensational. Granted, it requires more preparation, but the payoff is worth it.

After the subtraction has been performed and the number revealed, you can use a more dramatic approach in predicting the dictionary word. Instead of writing down your prediction and handing it to a spectator, you can produce a sealed envelope from somewhere in the room and hand it to a spectator. When the spectator opens the envelope, she will remove a slip of paper to see that the word matches the appropriate word in the dictionary.

Oh, come on, reader! It's only nine envelopes that you have to place around the room! All you have to do is remember where each envelope is hidden. If you need a cheat sheet, simply write down the location of each envelope on a small slip of paper. When the subtracted number has been announced, glance at the sheet to see the location of the proper envelope. It is not as difficult as it seems.

The audience might suspect that you have more than one envelope hidden around the room, but that will confuse them more. After all, you couldn't possibly have an envelope for each word in the dictionary, could you? They are not aware that you memorized only nine words.

A similar option would be to produce the envelope *after* the demonstration is over. Just imagine the impact on the audience if the following occurred:

- The three-digit number is chosen, reversed, and subtracted ...
- You write your prediction on a piece of paper in plain view of the audience ...
- The word is located in the dictionary, matching your word ...
  And then ...
- You nonchalantly walk over to the corner of the room and remove an envelope from under the cat's food dish. The audience is truly confounded when they see that the word in the envelope matches the word in the dictionary.

13

Carbon Copy

DIFFICULTY LEVEL: ◆◆◆◆◆
IMPACT: ✱✱✱✱✱
PARTNER: NO OR YES (TWO VERSIONS)
PREPARATION: CONSIDERABLE PRACTICE

Overview

Here is a demonstration that is sure to make your audience's knees buckle.

I am going to present to you two methods to execute this demonstration. The first requires the mind reader to use a sleight of hand technique and can be performed independently. Personally I prefer the second option, although it is a lot riskier and requires the assistance of a partner.

Which version is best for you? Read them both and decide.

The Premise

The mind reader selects three subjects from the audience to participate in a demonstration. He informs the subjects that he will be asking each of them a question and then writing down their responses on a small slip of paper.

He then asks the first subject to name a color. When the participant answers, the mind reader writes the response on his paper.

The second subject is asked to name a type of car, and the last subject is asked to name a U.S. state. After they respond, the mind reader writes their answers on the same slip of paper. This slip of paper is handed to one of the participants.

At this point in the demonstration, the mind reader slowly pulls out a wallet from a jacket that is draped over a chair. Very slowly and deliberately he unfolds the wallet to reveal a zippered compartment. In plain view of the audience, the mentalist opens the zipper. He then reaches his fingers in and produces a folded slip of paper with writing on it. He hands the paper to another participant and asks her to read it aloud to the audience. To the astonishment of the spectators, the slip of paper names the same color, car, and state that were selected by the audience members.

Unfathomable, you say? You should know better than that by now!

The Solution

Option #1:

In this method, the secret is to use two slips of paper. Each time a participant answers a question, write the same answer on each piece of paper. So when all three participants have answered their questions, you will have two slips of paper with identical information.

If you decide to use this option, you will need to make sure there is some distance between you and your audience. In other demonstrations, it is perfectly acceptable to have audience members right next to you during your performance. In "Carbon Copy," you must be standing several feet in front of a seated audience. This way, you can write the answers on a flat surface, above the audience's eye level. This will ensure that the audience does not see you writing on two slips of paper.

The first piece of paper is to be quickly and discreetly folded and secretly stored in your palm (under your pinkie and ring finger). You will be able to accomplish this as soon as you finish writing the last response. Simply take an extra second to fold the paper, pretending that you are still writing.

Are you with me or are your eyes glazed over? It gets a little confusing here, so make sure you understand everything up to this point. I'll be happy to wait while you reread the last three paragraphs.

Back? Okay, let's continue:

Once the first slip of paper is secure under your fingers, pick up the second slip and hand it to a participant. After producing a wallet from your jacket pocket, you unzip a compartment. Then you reach your fingers into the wallet compartment and slide the hidden slip of paper to your two front fingers, pretending that you pulled it from the compartment. Then hand the slip of paper to a participant to be read aloud for the audience.

As I mentioned, this technique requires considerable practice. Be cautioned: The slightest misstep and the demonstration is blown.

Option #2:

This method is very sneaky, which is probably why I like it better. While you are conducting the demonstration, your partner is off to the side, conversing with other people, pretending not to be paying attention to your performance.

As each participant responds, you record his or her answers on a piece of paper. At the same time, your partner is also recording their answers on an identical piece of paper. When all three subjects have responded, you begin a dialogue with the audience about ESP to keep their attention focused on you.

While you are conversing with the audience, your partner secretly folds her slip of paper and places it in a compartment in a wallet. Then she slips the wallet into a pocket in your jacket, which is hanging on a chair, off to the side of the audience.

Why will this work? Because the audience has no clue that your jacket will have anything to do with this demonstration. Why on earth would they even be looking at your jacket? Do you think that someone in the audience will say to themselves, "Hmm, I better keep an eye on this jacket in case someone tries to slip a wallet with a piece of paper into it"? Of course not!

As long as your partner casually places the slip of paper in the wallet and then nonchalantly places the wallet in the jacket, no one will catch on to your devious plot.

 ### Tips & Techniques

One time, I witnessed a mind reader perform this demonstration in front of an audience of 500 people. He used a transparently obvious, but nevertheless fun, way to present this demonstration. He began by saying, "Robert, please come down to the stage for the next part of my performance."

Although my name is Robert, I never for a moment suspected that he was inviting me to join him. After a few seconds of silence, the mind reader started looking through the audience and asked, "Robert, where are you? Don't be shy! Come on up here." Several more seconds of silence elapsed. I looked around the room; no one was getting up from their seat. Finally, I decided to stand up. After all, my name is Robert!

Once I stood, the mind reader looked at me and said, "There you are, Robert! Come on down and join me." Always willing to play along, I walked in front of the stage, where the mind reader indicated. He then proceeded to call two more spectators in a similar fashion.

Impressive? Not really—but fun anyway. It's not as if he took a big risk asking for a Robert in the audience. Out of 500 people, there must be at least a few in the crowd. Let's face it, if he wanted to impress people, he would have asked for a Nika or a Miss Horak or a Dr. Andrea Schwartz. Of course, you certainly do not have to call names at random for this demonstration to be effective.

If you use Option #1, make sure you are well rehearsed. Writing the answers on two slips of paper discreetly requires practice and finesse. Once you master the technique of folding the slip of paper and hiding it under your pinkie and ring finger, you are practically home free. Creating the illusion that you produced the slip of paper from the wallet is virtually undetectable if executed smoothly.

You can also try using a piece of carbon paper and placing it between the two slips of paper. This way you will not have to write the answers twice. Just make sure that you dispose of the carbon paper before the demonstration is completed.

The tremendous impact that this demonstration has on the audience is well worth the risk of being discovered. One word of advice: Have your car parked outside and running in case you have to make a mad dash out of the premises.

*C*onspiracy!

14

DIFFICULTY LEVEL: ✦✦✦✦✦
IMPACT: ✳✳✳✳✳
PARTNER: YES—A CONSPIRATOR!
PREPARATION: NONE

Overview

As you have seen from previous chapters, I have no morals. There are practically no depths to which I will not stoop in order to fool my audience into thinking I can read their minds. Having said that, I can now tell you that I have grave reservations in presenting this next chapter; for I—yes, even I—believe that it tests the very limits of human decency.

It is this: Working with a plant in the audience. No, I am not talking about a Canadian fern or a Southern lily shrub. What I am suggesting is using a human plant in the audience as a conspirator. A conspirator is different than a partner. You see, the audience is

75

aware that your partner is in on the secret with you. A conspirator appears to be just another member of the audience, but is actually working in concert with you to fool the audience.

I do not blame you if you fall into a fit of righteous indignation and throw this book into the trash. I am deeply ashamed to bring up such deceit to such a decent, moral, and upstanding person such as you.

Oh ... still reading are you? Haven't burned the book just yet? Well, in that case, let's explore a fun demonstration that employs the use of a conspirator.

The Premise

Do you remember earlier in the book I discussed the One-Up Principle? "Conspirator" is a stunning example of this ingenious technique. Through the use of a "shill," this amazing feat eliminates the guesswork associated with the One-Up Principle.

By allowing the audience to contribute open-ended information, the impact of "Conspirator" can be staggering.

The mind reader or an assistant distributes pencils and slips of paper to audience members. The number of participants is determined by how much time the mind reader would like to devote to this demonstration. The audience members are then asked to write something on a piece of paper. This can be as specific or as general as desired.

For the sake of this exercise, let's select historic figures. The audience will each write down a famous person from history. It could be someone they would like to meet or perhaps someone they would like to have been. When the names have been recorded and the slips of paper have been folded twice, they are collected and placed in a shoebox.

The shoebox is then brought up to the mind reader at the performing area. When the room is silent, the mind reader takes the first folded slip and holds it against his forehead. After a few seconds of concentrating, he announces to the audience what was written on the paper.

To the audience's astonishment, the mind reader is correct. This is repeated as many times as the mind reader desires, and each time, yields the same results.

The Solution

Prior to performing this demonstration, you will have to make an arrangement with a conspirator. If the category is going to be historic names, then you must find out what name he will be writing on his slip of paper. Once you know this, the rest of the demonstration is a breeze. For the sake of this explanation, let's assume that your conspirator selected Abraham Lincoln (my personal favorite).

After all of the names have been deposited in the shoebox, you will begin pulling out slips of paper and guessing what was written on each one. Of course, using the One-Up Principle, you will start with the conspirator's name, Abraham Lincoln—even though you did not pull out his entry.

After pulling out a folded slip of paper and holding it to your forehead, you announce to the crowd that the name written on the paper is Abraham Lincoln. You ask who in the crowd is a fan of our 16th president. The audience will be impressed as your shill confesses that he is the one who wrote Honest Abe.

Just to verify the answer, you will casually open the slip of paper. Although you nod in satisfaction that you got it right, you see that the name was not Abraham Lincoln. Instead, it was—let's say—Joan of Arc. Of course, you are the only one who can see this. Once the crowd quiets down and it is time to select another name, you pull out the next slip of paper and hold it to your forehead. You then announce that the name is Joan of Arc.

I think you can see where this is going. Each time you say a name, you open the slip of paper to verify your answer. This allows you to see the next answer.

Tips and Techniques

This is another demonstration that allows you to use showmanship and comedy to spice up the performance. When holding a slip of paper to your forehead, you can pretend that you are attempting to visualize what is written on the paper by falling into an exaggerated psychic trance replete with head bobbing, off-key chanting, etc. Try something like:

77

"Oh Great Spirit of Dementia come to me and give me the power to see the words written on this paper. I summon thee to channel your mystical powers into the sacred shoebox ..."

Instead of simply announcing the name on the slip of paper, you can allude to it by providing the audience with vague clues, and gradually leading up to the answer, similar to the technique described in "The Name Game" earlier in the book.

There is one situation that you must try to avoid. If you were to select your conspirator's piece of paper, the demonstration would end immediately. To avoid this, there is a very simple solution. After writing the answer and folding up the paper, have your conspirator draw a small dot on both sides of the paper before handing it in. This way you can glance down in the shoebox and avoid selecting his slip of paper until the end.

If you wish to stop the demonstration, simply look for the paper with the dot on it and make that your last one. This way if the audience wants to inspect the slips of paper, you have nothing to hide. Each of the names you mentioned will be written on the slips of paper you selected.

In any event, it is always a good idea to keep the used slips of paper out of the audience's view. There's no sense in risking the effectiveness of this demonstration by carelessly leaving the slips of paper out in the open.

15

The Wizard

DIFFICULTY LEVEL: ◆◆◆◆◆
IMPACT: ✳✳✳✳✳
PARTNER: YES
PREPARATION: EXTENSIVE REHEARSAL

Overview

This is, in my humble opinion, the single greatest demonstration ever created. It is certainly the most baffling and is guaranteed to leave audiences large and small stunned beyond belief. When this demonstration was first performed for me, I had to do a considerable amount of pleading to learn the secret. I was so dumbfounded, that I couldn't rest until I learned how it was performed. It took every ounce of persuasion, coercion, negotiating, and threatening I could muster to discover the well-kept secret.

The only reason that I mention this to you is because I know how it feels. Whenever I perform this demonstration, I understand the anguish experienced by the audience members. I can empathize with the uncontrollable yearn to know how it was performed. Yes, I am aware of the audience's unstoppable quest to learn the secret. I understand, because I have been there.

So, when I perform "The Wizard," I try to be compassionate to my naive, answer-hungry audience. After the demonstration is over, I allow them to beg for a short time, but then I remove myself from their presence because there is only so much whining and pleading a grown man can take.

In any event, I now present to you, in its entirety, the finest, most dazzling mind reading demonstration known to mankind, "The Wizard."

The Premise

The mind reader announces that he has a friend, called the Wizard, who is perhaps the greatest mentalist of all time. To prove it, an audience member selects a card from a borrowed, well-shuffled deck and announces it to the spectators. The mind reader then picks up a telephone and dials a number. Within a few seconds, the mind reader speaks to the Wizard and asks him to identify the secret card. At this point, the telephone is put on speaker mode—or if that is not possible—a member of the audience gets on the telephone and says hello. The Wizard miraculously identifies the correct card.

Each time the demonstration is repeated (oh believe me, they will insist you repeat it), the mind reader says the *same exact thing!* Even though the cards change, the words that the mind reader uses to communicate with the Wizard remain constant. They are as follows:

"Hello, may I speak to the Wizard, please?"

"Hello, Wizard?"

"What is the card?"

The same dialogue each time—and each time the same result. A flawless demonstration that leaves the audience breathless every time.

You can't believe it, you say? Well get ready. You are about to learn the secret to this startling classic.

The Solution

It is rather amusing to hear of some of the theories the audience has when trying to figure out the secret to this demonstration. One of my favorites is that I have 52 friends, each representing a different card in the deck. When I hear which card has been selected, I simply call that friend who says his designated card. This assumes, of course, that I even have 52 friends. I don't think I even know 52 people.

Another theory is that when I dial the telephone number, I press the buttons in such a way to indicate the card. People give me much more credit than I deserve.

The answer is much less complicated that that. In fact, it is remarkably simple. Keep in mind, that when a mind reader and his partner exchange clues, it is generally the partner who is transmitting the clues to the mind reader. I think that the reason people have such a hard time figuring out how this demonstration is performed is because in this case, the system is reversed.

Even though you are regarded as the mind reader, in this demonstration, you are actually acting as the partner. Remember, it is the Wizard who is identifying the card, not you. Knowing this, it becomes much clearer that the code is indeed being transmitted from the mind reader to the Wizard.

But how is this possible? After all, the mind reader is saying *the same phrases each time!* If he were transmitting clues, wouldn't he have to change what he says?

The answer to that, reader, is no!

Here's how it works:

You, as the mind reader, ask to borrow a deck from the host of the party. This is to ensure that the audience does not suspect that the deck has been prearranged. The deck is then given to a spectator who shuffles the cards thoroughly. In fact, a second spectator can also shuffle the cards. Once the audience is satisfied that the cards are completely mixed, the deck is placed on the table.

What makes this demonstration even more spectacular is that you never handle the cards. From the audience's point of view, this eliminates the possibility that you are doing something sneaky.

Another audience member is asked to fan out the cards and select one from the deck. Once this is accomplished, she holds the chosen card up to the audience so everyone has a chance to view it. You then ask the spectator to announce the card. For the sake of this explanation, let's assume that the card chosen was a seven of clubs.

Once this happens, you go into a monologue about the Wizard and his special powers. When the challenge of the demonstration has been established, you then—in plain view of everyone—pick up the telephone and dial a secret number.

When the person on the other end picks up and says "Hello," you then say:

"Hello, may I speak to the Wizard, please."

This is a clue to the "Wizard" that he is needed to help in this demonstration. The Wizard then begins to recite the card numbers: Ace, two, three, four, etc. While the Wizard counts through the cards, the audience assumes that you are waiting in silence while the Wizard is being called to the telephone.

When the Wizard reaches seven, you say:

"Hello, Wizard?"

When the audience hears this, they will simply think that the Wizard has said "Hello," and that you are verifying that it is indeed the Wizard on the telephone. In reality, the reason that you said "Hello, Wizard?" is to alert the Wizard that he has reached the secret card.

Does that make sense? The reader counts off card numbers in order starting from the ace. When he reaches the secret card, you alert him by saying your cue: "Hello, Wizard?"

The Wizard now knows that the card is a seven, and then proceeds to try to identify the suit. The Wizard begins stating the names of the suits: "seven of hearts, seven of diamonds, seven of clubs ..."

When the Wizard reaches clubs, you interrupt him and say, "What is the card?"

At this point, the Wizard knows that the card is a seven of clubs. You can then put the Wizard on speakerphone or hand the receiver to a spectator in the audience. The Wizard identifies the correct card, and the audience, in unison, gasps from witnessing such a feat of black magic.

Preparation

"The Wizard" requires perfect timing and execution to be successful. This can be accomplished with a quick-minded partner and a little practice.

The first thing to remember is that time is of the essence. Keep in mind that after you say, "Hello, may I speak to the Wizard, please?," there will be a pause. The reason that there is a pause is because the partner on the other end of the telephone will be reciting cards (ace, two, three, etc.). As I mentioned, the audience will think that this pause is merely because the person answering the telephone is alerting the Wizard that there is a phone call for him. The audience will excuse a few seconds, but anything beyond that will begin to look suspicious.

The next part of the demonstration is even more time-sensitive. When you say, "Hello, Wizard?" there is another pause. This pause is due to the fact that the Wizard is now listing the different suits.

But why is the audience willing to accept the fact that there is a pause here? Shouldn't it take less than a second for the conversation to continue? A way to solve this problem is to make it appear as if it is difficult to hear the Wizard. Also, it is extremely important for your partner to say the suits quickly to make this pause as short as possible. The Wizard should include the card number as well, though, to make sure he is on the right number. If the card is a seven but you didn't stop him in time, the Wizard will realize this after you don't say, "What is the card?" while he's rattling off "eight of diamonds, eight of spades ...," and he'll then try the sevens.

So, timing is everything. Your partner must be fully trained to spring into action as soon as he hears the phrase, "Hello, may I speak to the Wizard, please?" You must practice enough so that he is conditioned to be ready at all times.

Sometimes when many months go by without performing this demonstration, problems can arise. It has happened on more than one occasion that my partner experienced a complete mental lapse. Just imagine attempting to perform this feat in front of a room full of skeptical people. After giving the cue and asking to speak to the Wizard, all that I heard on the other line was whining. "Oh, it's been so long since I've done this. I don't remember what to do. Am I supposed to be giving clues or something?"

What can you do? Nothing, except stand there with a moronic grin on your face. It's not like you can freeze the audience and review with your partner how the demonstration is performed. All that can be done is hope that your partner comes to his senses.

You must also have excellent timing to pull this demonstration off correctly. When your partner is counting off numbers, you must be ready to give the clue at the precise moment. The cards should be read at a brisk pace so if you are even a fraction of a second too fast or too slow, your partner will guess the wrong card.

This is why "The Wizard" must be practiced repeatedly until it is second nature for the mind reader and the partner. Of course, several people can be trained as partners to ensure that someone will be available when it is time to perform. In fact, even the mind reader himself can act as partner if he were to ever receive the call asking for the Wizard.

At this point, you know enough to perform this demonstration and mystify your family and friends. If you would like to enhance this incredible feat, the next section will describe, in detail, ways that you can make this innovative demonstration even more unforgettable.

The Setup

"The Wizard" is a unique mind reading presentation and is perfect for a long, suspenseful buildup. A great way to begin the demonstration is to talk about an acquaintance—or better yet—an associate of yours. He is called the Wizard and lives atop a mountain peak in a remote village in Tibet. He is a very talented mentalist and extremely dedicated to his craft.

In fact, all he does day in and day out is sit by his telephone waiting for common folk to call and ask for his prediction. Through scorching heat, blizzards, and torrential rains he remains at his post, staring into space, knowing everything.

Today that silence will be broken. You will be contacting the Wizard to unleash his incredible mental powers. You then proceed with the selection of the card.

It is a wise precaution to mention that the Wizard's wife lives with him on top of the mountain, so that when you ask to speak to the Wizard, they will assume that Mrs. Wizard answered the telephone.

Tips & Techniques

If, by some chance, you should make a mistake, hang up. Do not attempt to say "No" or "That's not it" or—the worst thing you could possibly say: "Go back." Just let it go. Pretend the reception was getting worse and you lost the Wizard on the other end.

If you dial a wrong number, or if your partner asks you to call back in ten minutes, hang up immediately and have the audience select another card. This is because people are suspicious and suspect that the first call you made was some sort of clue.

If repeating this demonstration, don't break the pattern of using the same words each time. It will seem as if you are giving clues if you do not stick to the same script.

When you call, pretend that you are dialing a lot of numbers. It is amusing when it appears as if you are dialing 30 numbers to make a long distance call. If you are performing this demonstration at a friend's house, it always gets a reaction when you announce that you will need to use his phone to make a call—to Tibet.

When you have performed this demonstration a number of times and feel confident that you can execute it correctly each time, you may want to work on developing clues to facilitate the process. One way that this could be accomplished is to ever-so-slightly alter a word or intonation in the delivery of the set phrases. Here are some examples:

- If the card is an eight or higher, instead of saying, "Hello, *may* I speak to the Wizard, please," say, "Hello, *can* I speak to the Wizard, please." The audience will surely not notice this subtle difference.
- If the card is a picture, put the "please" before the word "speak" instead of at the end of the sentence.
- If the card is a heart, say "Hi" instead of "Hello."

These methods are certainly not needed, as the demonstration can stand on its own merits. It is conceivable that you could have a separate phrase for each suit, but that would take far too much time devising this system, and most people generally have more productive things to do with their lives.

This demonstration can also be performed without a deck of cards. It will seem just as random if a member of the audience is allowed to simply name a card from the deck. If you decide to select a card in this manner, you will notice that certain cards are repeated quite often. To make this demonstration seem even more spectacular, you can have a quick clue for the two most popular selections: the ace of spades and the queen of hearts.

If you have a quick clue, it will look like a miracle. For example, if your clue for the ace of spades was "Card," all you would have to do is pick up the telephone and when your partner answers, simply say, "Card," then hand the phone to a spectator. The audience will be dumbfounded that this could be accomplished by using just one word.

When you hand the telephone to a spectator to speak to the Wizard, your partner has a perfect opportunity to ham it up. Instead of simply revealing the card, your partner can have some fun by getting into the character of the mystical, eccentric, bizarre Wizard.

At this point in the demonstration, the audience usually thinks that this is the time when the Wizard tries to discover the card. They do not realize that the identity of the secret card has already been discovered, so whatever the Wizard does from this point on is just for show.

First, a fake voice is mandatory. Whoever heard of a Wizard without a bizarre voice? Your partner can either opt for the spooky low voice that draws the words out slowly, or perhaps a high squeaky one that is practically unbearable to listen to.

The Wizard can begin to ask a series of completely unrelated questions, such as:
• "What is your favorite television program?"
• "What did you have for dinner last night?"
• "What color are your socks?"

86

Then, based upon this information, the Wizard renders a guess. The spectators will be truly impressed that the Wizard can identify the card just from asking those questions!

When you hand the telephone to a spectator to hear the Wizard's prediction, there is a tendency for the subject to remain silent and wait for the Wizard to begin speaking. Well, your partner is no mind reader so make sure you tell the subject to say "Hello" to the Wizard upon handing over the phone.

Sometimes, being under pressure, your partner may accidentally begin reading the cards in reverse order (ace, king, queen, etc.). Just be aware that this is a common mistake and you shouldn't let it throw you off.

Finally, after your partner has correctly identified the card, he should immediately hang up the telephone. It is unfortunate that your partner never gets to hear the reaction from the audience, but it is a much better effect. If your partner does not immediately hang up the telephone, the audience member will certainly pester him to learn the secret. This would diminish the impact of the demonstration.

When you repeat this demonstration for the same audience, you could use a short cut. If you call your partner back a few seconds later to guess another card, your partner can answer the telephone and immediately begin counting cards (ace, two, three, etc.)—without waiting to hear you say, "Hello, may I speak to the Wizard, please." This cuts out a step and reduces the time it takes to identify the card. The rest of the demonstration would be performed as described above.

A Great Variation

A fun twist to this all-time classic is made possible because of modern technology. By using caller ID, your partner can make a tremendous impact on the audience. Here's how it works:

You begin the demonstration as described above. The variation comes into play after your partner names the suits. When the Wizard reaches the correct suit, instead of saying your usual line ("What is the card?"), you will simply hang up the telephone. This will signal to your partner that he reached the appropriate suit.

After hanging up, you announce to the spectators that you are sorry, but you will be unable to perform this demonstration because the connection to Tibet is too weak.

This is the fun part! Since your partner has caller ID, he knows the telephone number of where you are! After a moment goes by your partner calls the telephone number. The hostess of the party answers the call and is shocked to find out that it is the Wizard who is calling. He then proceeds to tell her the card that was selected moments earlier.

If your partner does not possess caller ID, this same effect can be achieved by dialing *69. By doing this, the telephone company will state the number of the last incoming call. In some cases, dialing *69 will automatically dial the number of the last incoming call. You should be aware that there is usually a charge for this service.

If you plan ahead and your partner is expecting the call, he can pick up the phone and start saying cards immediately. The audience will think the phone is still ringing. At the right card you say "Hello, Wizard?" Then you hang up when the right suit comes up. You've identified the card by just saying two words. Even better is to call and have your forewarned partner pick up the phone and start saying cards. You say something like, "The Wizard lives in a large house and sometimes it takes him a while to answer" when your partner gets to the right card. The audience doesn't know he has picked up. Then you hang up at the correct suit. The spectators think you've said nothing to the wizard, but he calls back with the correct card.

Cheating

As with many demonstrations, cheating is very much encouraged—if you can get away with it. Here is a great way to cheat when performing "The Wizard":

When performing this demonstration in front of a room full of people, there is generally a lot of commotion and distractions. This is especially true after it has been performed once already, and people are discussing it in bewilderment. Of course, people will be clamoring for you to do it again. This is a perfect time to be sneaky.

While the audience is trying to decide on a new card, you will have the telephone in your hand. Discreetly push the redial button.

When your partner answers the telephone, he will hear the demonstration being discussed and immediately understand what is happening. When the audience agrees upon a card, you can say it back to them, just to confirm their selection. Your partner will hear this and be ready to "guess" the card immediately, without any clues.

You would then pretend to dial the telephone, and within a few seconds, simply say, "What is the card?" You then hand off the telephone to a spectator, or put the Wizard on speakerphone, and let the demonstration play out as before.

Yes, I know, your mommy told you it's bad to cheat and lie. Take it from me, it isn't.

*W*izard *J*unior

DIFFICULTY LEVEL: ◆◆◆◆◆
IMPACT: ✳✳✳✳✳
PARTNER: YES
PREPARATION: MODERATE REHEARSAL

Overview

This is a remarkable demonstration that rivals "The Wizard" in audience impact. I call this miracle "Wizard Junior" because it is quite similar in concept. Unlike "The Wizard," which can be performed several times for the same audience, this demonstration can be performed only once.

The Premise

As in "The Wizard," the phone plays a key role in this demonstration. Only this time the mind reader is completely out of the loop. The mind reader announces that he has a psychic friend in another location. This friend will be able to guess a card that was selected.

A spectator is asked to choose a card from a borrowed deck and announce it to the audience. Once this is accomplished the mind reader pulls out a slip of paper from his pocket with a telephone number written on it. He then hands it to another spectator. This spectator dials the number and speaks with the mind reader's friend.

The spectator asks the psychic friend what the card is, and miraculously, the friend gets it right on the money.

Sounds too good to be true? Read on!

The Solution

The best part of this demonstration is that the mind reader is entirely out of the loop. He never touches the deck of cards. He never handles the telephone. He never speaks to his friend. It's diabolical!

Let's go over this demonstration step by step:

You, the mind reader, ask the host for a deck of cards. A randomly selected spectator is asked to choose a card from the deck and announce it to the audience.

Once everyone in the room is aware of the card, you then hand another spectator a piece of paper with a number on it. As you do this, you tell the spectator the name of your friend, who is actually your partner. *The name of the friend is the key!*

Through a simple code, the answer to the secret card lies in the name that you give to the spectator. So when your partner answers the telephone and hears what name is being used, she immediately knows the card that was selected.

The code is easy to master with a little practice. For the sake of this example, let's assume that the card selected was the six of diamonds.

The first name of your "friend" will indicate the suit of the card and will either begin with an S (spade), C (club), H (heart), or D (diamond). For our example, the six of diamonds, we could use the name Donna.

Your friend's last name will indicate the number of the card. The first letter of the last name corresponds with a letter in the alphabet. If the name begins with an A, then your friend knows the card is an ace. If the name begins with a B, this indicates that the card is a 2, C is a 3, D is a 4, and so on.

So, in our example, the spectator would ask to speak with Donna Findlay because the "D" in Donna stands for diamonds, and the "F" in Findlay indicates the number 6 because it is the sixth letter in the alphabet.

Tips & Techniques

As you can see, this demonstration can work only once for the same audience. This is because it would seem awfully suspicious if you attempted to repeat this feat and have a spectator dial the same number, asking for a different person. It would be so obvious that you might as well have the spectator ask to speak to the four of clubs.

I presented you the code in its most basic form. The problem here is that this simple code is decipherable. It is entirely possible that the audience will pool their heads together and strongly suspect that Donna stands for diamonds.

Of course, as in "The Wizard," the most foolproof solution would be to have 52 friends who were each assigned a card. These friends would all have to stay home and sit by the telephone in case you decided to perform this demonstration. In the event that you don't have 52 friends who are willing to dedicate their lives to sitting next to a telephone all day long for the sake of your demonstration, then you can try something a little more practical.

If you alter the code slightly, you can make it nearly impossible for anyone to figure out your secret. The part of the code that is most vulnerable to being deciphered is the first name of the friend. *Donna* just may be too transparent a clue for *Diamond*. And once they figure out that much, it is just a matter of time before they crack the code of the last name.

My suggestion is to simply work out a set of names with your partner beforehand. These names do not need to have any relevance to anything, other than that they each represent a particular suit. Just make sure that the names you select do not bear any resemblance to the suits in the deck. In fact, it would be best if none of the letters matched the suit letters at all!

If you prefer, you can simply develop a code where the "D" for diamonds will be the *second letter* in the first name, or perhaps the last letter.

This code could also be used for the last name, making it nearly impossible for the audience to catch on. Instead of having the first letter of the last name correspond with the number, use the *second letter* of the name.

For example, if the card were a six of diamonds, you would just make sure that the *second letter* of the last name begins with an "F" (F = 6). So the last name of your "friend" could be Aflack.

Even the most astute observer would have a difficult time drawing any association between the friend's name and the selected card.

In reality, it is very rare that someone will decipher this demonstration, even if you use simple codes.

As in "The Wizard," your partner has the option of stating the card right away or building suspense by prolonging the demonstration. Again, your partner can ask irrelevant questions to make the audience think that the spectator's answers somehow give your "friend" clues to determine the secret card. It can be quite humorous if the questions become rather personal.

Inevitably, the audience will suspect that you are in cahoots with the audience member who speaks to your partner on the telephone. They will accuse the spectator of simply pretending that the person on the other end of the telephone guessed the secret card. This is why you must select a spectator who is beyond reproach. Choose the person who would never be suspected of collaborating with you to trick the audience.

Conclusion

Ah, what an experience we have shared together. I feel like a tremendous weight has been lifted from my shoulders. No longer must I bear the burden of keeping these secrets to myself. This responsibility has been passed on to you.

Now you know the secrets of mind reading. Just make sure that your friends and relatives don't get their hands on this book. To be safe, it may be a good idea to buy every copy of *Mystifying Mind Reading Tricks* from your local bookstores.

Do you feel enriched by the lessons you have learned? I certainly hope so. May you enjoy baffling friends and strangers in the years to come. If you have any questions regarding these demonstrations, or if you would like to share some of your mind reading experiences, feel free to send me an e-mail at MindReaderESP@aol.com. I look forward to hearing from you!

But, after reading this book and developing your mind reading skills, I suppose that you already knew what my e-mail address was.

You did?

How did you *do* that!?

STACEY
ABRAMS

STACEY ABRAMS

CHAMPION OF DEMOCRACY

DR. ARTIKA R. TYNER

LERNER PUBLICATIONS ◆ MINNEAPOLIS

Lerner Publications Company
An imprint of Lerner Publishing Group, Inc.
241 First Avenue North
Minneapolis, MN USA 55401

For reading levels and more information, look up this title at www.lernerbooks.com.

Image credits: REUTERS/Phil McCarten/Alamy Stock Photo, p. 2; AP Photo/Brynn Anderson, p. 6; Alyssa Pointer/Atlanta Journal-Constitution via AP, pp. 8, 11; AP Photo/John Bazemore, pp. 9, 32; Brian Cahn/ZUMA Wire/TNS/Alamy Stock Photo, p. 10; Bob Andres/Atlanta Journal-Constitution via AP, pp. 13, 19, 33; Jonathan Goldberg/Alamy Stock Photo, p. 14; AP Photo, pp. 15, 16; Mike Levitt/Invision for Girl Scouts via AP, p. 18; Andre Jenny/Alamy Stock Photo, p. 21; Atlanta Journal-Constitution via AP, pp. 23, 25; Nick Arroyo/Atlanta Journal-Constitution via AP, p. 24; David L. Harris/Library of Congress (LC-DIG-ppmsca-70889), p. 27; f11photo/Shutterstock.com, p. 28; Sandra Baker/Alamy Stock Photo, p. 29; AP Photo/ David Goldman, p. 31; Bill Clark/CQ Roll Call via AP, p. 34; Michele and Tom Grimm/Alamy Stock Photo, p. 35; REUTERS/Brendan McDermid/Alamy Stock Photo, p. 36; 7partparadigm/ United States Department of the Interior/Wikimedia Commons, p. 37; AP Photo/Ben Gray, p. 38; Senate Television via AP, p. 39; 52nd NAACP Image Awards/BET/Getty Images, p. 40.

Cover: Jamie Lamor Thompson/Shutterstock.com.

Main body text set in Rotis Serif Std 55 Regular. Typeface provided by Adobe Systems.

Library of Congress Cataloging-in-Publication Data

Names: Tyner, Artika R., author.
Title: Stacey Abrams: champion of democracy / Dr. Artika R. Tyner.
Description: Minneapolis: Lerner Publications [2022] | Series: Gateway biographies | Includes bibliographical references and index. | Audience: Ages 9–14 | Audience: Grades 4–6 | Summary: "Stacey Abrams is a lawyer, entrepreneur, and voting rights activist. After working in government, she founded Fair Fight Action to improve voting access. Learn about Abrams's early life and what she plans to do next"–Provided by publisher.
Identifiers: LCCN 2021035870 (print) | LCCN 2021035871 (ebook) | ISBN 9781728441849 (library binding) | ISBN 9781728448787 (paperback) | ISBN 9781728444734 (ebook)
Subjects: LCSH: Abrams, Stacey—Juvenile literature. | Black women politicians—Georgia—Biography—Juvenile literature. | Politicians—Georgia—Biography—Juvenile literature. | Legislators—Georgia—Biography—Juvenile literature. | Suffrage—United States—History—21st century. | Black legislators—Georgia—Biography—Juvenile literature.
Classification: LCC F291.3.A27 T96 2022 (print) | LCC F291.3.A27 (ebook) | DDC 975.8/044092 [B]—dc23

LC record available at https://lccn.loc.gov/2021035870
LC ebook record available at https://lccn.loc.gov/2021035871

Manufactured in the United States of America
1-49939-49782-9/15/2021

TABLE OF CONTENTS

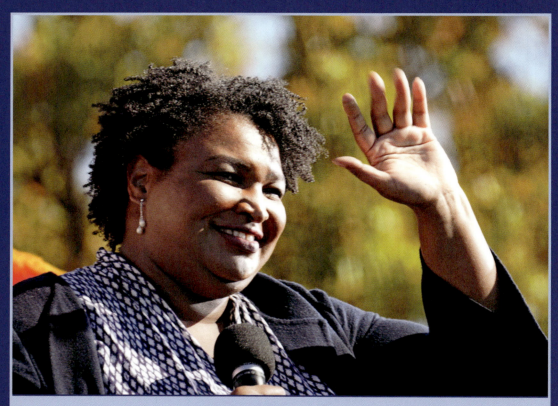

Stacey Abrams addresses supporters of Democratic presidential candidate Joe Biden in November 2020.

In November 2018, many eyes were on Georgia's gubernatorial race. The election saw Democrat Stacey Abrams face off against Republican Brian Kemp. As the final votes were counted, Kemp led Abrams by a little less than fifty thousand votes. Kemp beat Abrams to become the next governor of Georgia. It was one of the closest statewide races in recent US history.

The nation awaited a final concession speech from Abrams. She was known as a young, ambitious, and visionary leader. Many dreamed she would transform Georgia. During her campaign for governor, Abrams created a plan to increase funding for children's education. She wanted to expand access to health care for everyone. Her plans encouraged small business owners to grow, supported criminal justice reform, and aimed to improve access to mental health services.

After the results of Georgia's 2018 race for governor came in, Abrams voiced concerns that the race had not been conducted fairly.

Abrams sparked interest in voting and civic engagement across the nation. She reminded everyday people that their voices mattered. They could help to shape laws and policies on issues from immigration to criminal justice. They could serve their communities to transform local schools and economies. She challenged citizens to take action to build stronger communities and brighter futures.

On November 16, 2018, Abrams stood at a podium at her campaign's headquarters in Atlanta, Georgia. Her supporters gathered to listen, and people from across the nation and the world watched as the speech was broadcast. Abrams looked into the camera and began to speak, starting with the history of voting and democracy.

Abrams also referred to concerns that the race for governor was not conducted fairly. Kemp ran for office while he was Georgia's secretary of state. One of his duties was to oversee elections. This meant Kemp both oversaw and ran in the same election. During the race, his office removed over a half million voters from Georgia's registry. His office also blocked fifty-three thousand new voters from voting. These actions created challenges for voters hoping to register and cast their ballots.

Brian Kemp in November 2018

Many Georgia voters faced long lines on election day.

Voters in Georgia faced more difficulties on election day. Some polling places were closed, while others were short of paper ballots. Polling stations were overcrowded, and lines to vote were long. People waited in lines for hours, some for as many as eight. Others had their ballots thrown out if their signature did not match the one on their original voting registration card. Many were confused about how to vote by mail through an absentee ballot and how to vote in person. People were also given mixed messages. Abrams herself was initially told that she could not vote in person since she had requested an absentee ballot. But she had never applied to vote absentee. Voting machines malfunctioned. The list of issues continued to grow.

Abrams said that Georgia had failed its citizens. "More than 200 years into Georgia's democratic experiment, the state failed its voters," she said. "Let's be clear—this is not a speech of concession, because concession means to acknowledge an action is right, true or proper." She encouraged everyone to take a stand for democracy by ensuring fairness in elections and voting rights for all. She said the future of Georgia was in their hands.

Many believe the issues with the election caused Abrams to lose the election. Some believed they were examples of voter suppression, or strategies to intentionally

Abrams with her nephew, Cameron McLean, after casting her vote in 2018

make voting difficult. But Abrams still made history by running for governor of Georgia. She was the first Black woman to receive a nomination for governor by a major US political party.

Abrams had hoped this would be only one of a series of trailblazing moments. She would have been not only Georgia's first female Black governor but the first in the United States. And she would have been the first Democrat to win a statewide race in Georgia since 2000. But Abrams is still making history as she registers a record number of voters, supports the creation of better job opportunities, and works to ensure everyone is counted in the US Census.

Family Roots, Family Values

Stacey Abrams was born on December 9, 1973, in Madison, Wisconsin, to Robert and Carolyn Abrams. Stacey was their second child out of six. When Stacey was young, her family moved to the South. Stacey spent her early years in Gulfport, Mississippi. Her family lived in Gulfport until she reached middle school.

Stacey grew up with deep connections to her family. Her parents worked hard to build a strong and successful life for their children. Her father was a shipyard worker, and her mother was a head librarian. Though their family had little money, Stacey's parents taught all their children about the importance of high expectations. Stacey

Abrams and her parents as she began her campaign for governor in March 2018

and her siblings were encouraged to dream big, pursue their education, and serve their community. Stacey and her siblings learned from their mother the importance of reading and writing. The family enjoyed learning, watching PBS specials, and reading books together. As a childhood pastime, Stacey liked to read the encyclopedia. It was her opportunity to learn about a wide range of topics and unleash her imagination. She could travel the world and explore history. Also at an early age, Stacey discovered her gift for writing. She started writing and never stopped, going on to write several novels as an adult.

Modeling the way for their children, Stacey's parents were serious about education for themselves too. The family moved to Georgia so her parents could continue their schooling. Both attended Emory University and earned graduate degrees in divinity. Their strong belief in serving others led them to become United Methodist ministers.

Stacey's family experienced hard times. Yet they persevered. When they were unable to pay their bills, the water was cut off. Stacey's mother referred to this jokingly as "urban camping." No matter the challenges they faced, Stacey's parents reminded her that having nothing is no excuse for doing nothing.

Service was a big part of their lives. The family served in the community together. They volunteered at soup kitchens and helped the homeless. They volunteered together at prison outreach programs and at polling places during elections. Stacey and her siblings were taught three

The Abrams family prepared meals for those in need in kitchens like this one.

key values: go to school, go to church, and take care of one another. They also were assigned an important job. If they saw someone in need, Stacey and her siblings had to help that person.

The family also served in the community by promoting civic engagement and equal rights. Stacey's grandmother taught her the importance of voting. She reminded Stacey of Black people's long struggle for voting rights. In 1870 the Fifteenth Amendment

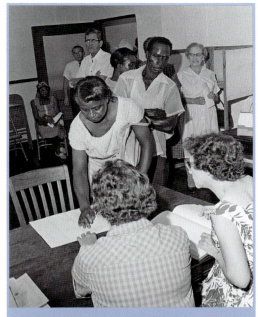

Black voters casting ballots in Mississippi in 1967

to the US Constitution granted Black men the right to vote. However, states then created laws to enforce racial segregation, or the separation of Black and white people. These Jim Crow laws included requiring people to take literacy tests and pay poll taxes to vote. One law called the grandfather clause said that people could vote only if their grandfather could vote before the Civil War. These laws intentionally created barriers to voting for Black men.

Black women fought in the movement for women's voting rights. They hoped their efforts would lead to not only gender equality but also to racial justice. The Nineteenth Amendment granted voting rights to women in 1920. But for Black women, the amendment's passage did not mean they could actually exercise these rights. In the face of restrictive voting laws, both Black men and women saw the harsh truth that the promise of equal rights did not include them.

Black people fought for their voting rights for generations. During the Civil Rights Movement, they marched and protested for justice. On March 7, 1965—later known as Bloody Sunday—voting rights activists organized a march from Selma, Alabama, to Montgomery, Alabama, to protest the unfair treatment of Black voters in the state. Future congressional representative John Lewis led more than six hundred people to march across the Edmund Pettus Bridge in Selma. They were brutally beaten by state troopers.

Finally, in 1965, the Voting Rights Act was

Martin Luther King Jr. (*right*) leads a march for voting rights in 1965 alongside fellow civil rights leader Ralph Abernathy (*left*).

signed into law. Stacey's grandmother voted for the first time three years later. She put on her best clothes to go to the polls. At first, she was afraid to cast her vote. She remembered how Black people had been beaten, sprayed with fire hoses, bitten by dogs, and even killed for trying to vote. But she overcame the fear of retribution by thinking about the future. She understood her vote was her power to make a difference, and she believed that she owed it to her children and the following generations to use that power. After that first vote in 1968, Stacey's grandmother never missed an election.

The Voting Rights Act of 1965

The Voting Rights Act of 1965 was signed into law by President Lyndon B. Johnson. It outlawed discriminatory practices that restricted access to voting. But in 2013, one piece of the act was struck down by the Supreme Court. This piece required states to earn outside approval to change certain voting practices. With this oversight, states had more difficulty creating laws intended to exclude certain voters. Without it, many believed creating discriminatory laws would become easier.

Unstoppable

Stacey learned early never to give up. In the mid-1980s she was selected by her Girl Scout troop leaders to represent Mississippi at a Girl Scouts national conference. Some community members were unhappy that a Black girl was selected. They tried to make sure that she didn't make it to the conference by changing her flight reservation and leaving her behind. But Stacey was unstoppable. She flew by herself to the national conference in Arizona.

Stacey's parents also helped to prepare her for the difficult road ahead. They did not want her to let adversity convince her to abandon her dreams. "Let other people

Girl Scouts aims to teach girls civic responsibility as well as leadership and practical skills.

Abrams's parents, the Reverend Robert Abrams (*front left*) and the Reverend Carolyn Abrams (*right*), continue to be big influences in her life.

tell you no," her father told her. "Never tell yourself no. If there's something you want, fight for it." This wisdom guided her studies and continues to guide her career. Stacey knew her destiny was greater than anyone could imagine. She learned to tell herself, *Yes, you can!*

The Girl Scouts experience and other experiences taught her to keep pressing forward during difficult challenges. During her campaign for governor, she reflected on the lessons she had learned: "There are going to be a lot of people who try to stop you from getting on that plane. There are a lot of people organizing themselves to make sure I land at the wrong destination. There are folks who don't think it's time for a Black woman to be governor of any state, let alone a state in the Deep South. But there's no wrong time for a Black woman to be in charge." During her race for governor, Abrams drew upon the strength she showed as a young girl. She kept her final destination in clear focus. She was determined to fight for justice and build a stronger Georgia.

Top of the Class

Stacey was an excellent student. When she was a junior in high school, she earned a high score on the PSAT. This precollege exam prepares students for the SAT. It also identifies top-performing students from across the nation. Based on her score, Stacey was selected for the Telluride Association Summer Program. This is a prestigious summer program for high-achieving youth. She attended the program with some of the brightest students in the nation.

The experience initially felt overwhelming. She realized the other students had had different privileges and access to opportunities than she had. It was difficult for her to compete, and she called her parents to ask if she could return home. But her parents made her complete the program. Stacey decided not to let anyone intimidate her and make her give up. She learned as much as she could from her peers.

After she finished the program, her ambition and confidence grew. She was determined to make her dreams come true. She later referenced the Bible to write,

"Proverbs tells us that iron sharpens iron. So too does ambition sharpen ambition. Dreams hone other dreams." The summer program prepared her for the future as she dared to dream bigger.

At eighteen Abrams graduated from Avondale High School in DeKalb County, Georgia, with honors. She was the highest-achieving student at her school and was named the valedictorian. In Georgia the governor sends a special invitation to high school valedictorians for a meeting at the governor's mansion. Abrams traveled to the other side of town with her parents to attend the special celebration. Her family could not afford a car, so they took a bus. A guard at the gate of the governor's mansion watched them as the bus pulled away. As Abrams and her family approached, he told them that they did not belong there.

Most states provide homes for their governors. This is the governor's mansion in Atlanta, Georgia.

Abrams's father confirmed that she was being recognized as one of the state's high school valedictorians. Her mother opened her purse and retrieved the invitation to try to show the guard. He ignored them and repeated that they did not belong there. Eventually, he looked at the list, saw Abrams's name, and allowed them to join the event. But the experience set the stage for Abrams's future career. She was determined to create opportunities where there was a true sense of community. She would help to create places where everyone knew that they belonged, that their voices mattered, and that they had the power to shape their destinies.

Spelman Bound

Abrams had an important decision to make: where she would attend college. She had spent most of her life in the South, but she wanted to go to school in the North. Her mother's dream had been to attend Spelman, a historically Black women's college in Atlanta, Georgia. But she could not afford to attend. Abrams's mother convinced her to apply to the prestigious college and make her unfulfilled dream a reality.

After Abrams was admitted to Spelman, she took a day to visit the school. Spelman is the oldest historically Black college for women. Abrams saw that the school was committed to inspiring Black women to change the world. She envisioned herself becoming part of a rich legacy of high-achieving Black women leaders. Though she had wanted to go to school in the North, she decided to attend Spelman.

Spelman College

Founded in 1881, Spelman College is one of a group of historically Black colleges and universities (HBCUs). These schools were created to educate Black students when many were barred from higher education. Spelman was founded specifically to educate and inspire Black women. Important women such as author Alice Walker, children's advocate Marian Wright Edelman, activist Bernice King, and business leader Rosalind Brewer graduated from Spelman.

Abrams at Spelman in 1992

While at Spelman, Abrams excelled academically. She emerged as a natural leader and used her voice to make a difference. She was named a Harry S. Truman Scholar in recognition of her academic success and commitment to public service. As a sophomore, she decided to become a student leader. She organized her campaign and was elected vice president of student government. During her junior year, she applied for the prestigious Rhodes scholarship. The scholarship allows students around the world to earn fully funded graduate degrees at the University of Oxford in England. Abrams was the first Black woman from Mississippi to be chosen as a candidate. Many told her that the distinction meant she was likely to succeed at the national level. But she was not chosen for the scholarship. She later reflected upon this experience, stating, "Losing prepares you for success." Abrams learned that she had to be willing to take a risk and strive to reach her goals. Losing the scholarship helped her to overcome the fear of failure.

Abrams was determined to stand up for what was right no matter what. Sometimes this meant taking risks and going up against powerful people. During Abrams's junior year of college, the first Black mayor of Atlanta, Maynard Jackson Jr., visited Spelman to hold a town hall. Abrams publicly challenged Jackson over his record on social justice issues. The move could have backfired, but instead, Jackson was impressed. He later created an Office of Youth Services

Maynard Jackson Jr. (*center*)

and hired Abrams to be a member of his team. She was the only undergraduate student on the staff, demonstrating her leadership skills and setting her apart from her peers.

In 1993 Abrams was selected as a youth speaker at the thirtieth anniversary of the March on Washington. She drew upon the leadership legacies of President Abraham Lincoln and Martin Luther King Jr. She challenged her listeners to focus on how young people could help to build a road to better jobs, justice, and peace. She dispelled the myth that young people had to wait to lead, insisting that age does not determine what someone can achieve. Abrams created a vision of shared partnerships between young people and adults in creating change. Future generations could not afford to wait for the promise of equal rights and justice to be realized. The work must be done today.

During her college years, Abrams launched her first voter registration campaign by recruiting her friends to vote. She convinced them of the importance of voting, emphasizing it as a key way to use your voice in a democratic society. Abrams also attended city council meetings and zoning meetings to study government and policy-making in action. She worked to have the Confederate emblem removed from the Georgia state flag. For many, the emblem is a reminder of racial terrorism and violence against Black people dating back to the Civil War and earlier. Her and others' advocacy led to the flag being changed. Each of these experiences provided Abrams with the tools to inspire, motivate, and organize others. She used these tools throughout her career.

The March on Washington

The March on Washington was in August 1963. Organized by civil rights leader A. Philip Randolph, the march's purpose was to demand good jobs and freedom for Black people. More than 250,000 people gathered in front of the Lincoln Memorial in Washington, DC. King delivered his famous "I Have a Dream" speech. Other prominent leaders in the Civil Rights Movement also spoke, including Bayard Rustin, National Association for the Advancement of Colored People president Roy Wilkins, John Lewis of the Student Non-Violent Coordinating Committee, organizer Daisy Bates, and actors Ossie Davis and Ruby Dee. Iconic singers such as Marian Anderson and Mahalia Jackson performed.

Abrams graduated with honors with a bachelor's degree in interdisciplinary studies (political science, economics, and sociology) and a minor in theater. Spelman provided her with a strong foundation to build her future. She decided to continue her studies and pursue a graduate degree.

The Young Lawyer

In line with her commitment to public service, Abrams earned a master's degree in public affairs from the Lyndon B. Johnson School of Public Affairs at the

The University of Texas's Lyndon B. Johnson School of Public Affairs is named after the thirty-sixth US president.

Yale University in New Haven, Connecticut, is one of the most prestigious schools in the US.

University of Texas at Austin. Her education there gave her the tools to transform government policies. She decided to attend Yale Law School to learn more about law and how to use it to create change. After graduating in 1999, she returned to Atlanta and became a tax attorney at the law firm Sutherland, Asbill & Brennan. From 1999 to 2003, she practiced tax law with a focus on tax-exempt organizations and public finance. At twenty-nine, Abrams was appointed the deputy city attorney for the City of Atlanta. She oversaw legal and policy analysis for the city's transportation and key economic development initiatives. She managed a team of more than twenty attorneys and paralegals.

Lawyers Leading Change

When Abrams decided to attend law school, she knew that lawyers have shaped the course of history. They can serve as leaders who seek justice and protect the rights of the people. Charles Hamilton Houston (1895–1950) is one lawyer who made a difference. He laid the groundwork for the case of *Brown v. Board of Education* (1954) that ended racial segregation in schools. Barbara Jordan (1936–1996) was a lawyer, professor, and public servant. She was the first Black woman elected to the Texas State Senate and the first southern Black woman elected to the US House of Representatives. She advocated for better wages and labor laws to protect workers.

Working for the People

Abrams's commitment to public service and the betterment of society compelled her to run for office. She was elected as a state representative in Georgia. She served eleven years in the Georgia House of Representatives, seven as the Democratic leader. In 2010 Abrams became the House minority leader for the Georgia General Assembly, making history again as the first woman from either party to do so. She was also the first Black woman to lead in the House.

Abrams remembered what she was taught as a little girl about service and helping others. She worked across the aisle with Republicans to serve the needs of the people of Georgia. She helped to prevent a large tax increase that would have created financial hardship for many Georgians. She helped to improve public transportation. She helped to save important scholarships for students in need. She worked with then Republican governor Nathan Deal to promote criminal justice reform.

Abrams is committed to helping people understand the power they have through voting. Before she ran for governor, she created the New Georgia Project, a voter registration organization. Between 2014 and 2016, her team helped more than two hundred thousand people of color register to vote.

Abrams speaks in Georgia's House of Representatives in 2016.

She continued to connect with people and learn their stories. She encouraged them to shape their destinies by becoming civically engaged. Abrams sought to create an atmosphere where all Georgians knew they belonged. Drawing upon her experience more than twenty years earlier of not being welcomed at the governor's mansion, she decided to open the gates of opportunity to everyone. No matter one's race, gender, class, or educational attainment, everyone would be included in building a more just and inclusive Georgia.

Abrams ran for governor of Georgia in 2018, losing by a narrow margin. The election was one of the closest statewide races in recent history. After the election, Abrams sat shiva for ten days. Shiva is a period of grief

Abrams inspired many in her fight to become Georgia's governor.

Abrams works at a Fair Fight phone bank in Atlanta in 2019.

and mourning in Judaism. She then began to strategize about her next move. She was determined not to allow what many believed were voter suppression tactics to influence an election again. She founded Fair Fight Action, a national voting rights organization, in Georgia.

Fair Fight focuses on democracy-building through the power of voting rights. The organization fights to end voter suppression and ensure accountability in elections. It uses three strategies. The first is litigation. Fair Fight files lawsuits when it believes that voters have been treated unfairly or that officials have behaved unlawfully. The second is legislation. The organization works to create policies that ensure everyone has equal access to the ballot box. The third is advocacy. Fair Fight works with communities to support civic engagement and voter participation. Through its efforts, the organization hopes to provide people with the tools to understand their voting rights and their important role in US democracy.

Another issue Abrams focuses on is the US Census. The Census is an effort to count every person living in the US. The count happens every ten years. The Census shapes the future of a community. It decides which communities receive federal funding, how much money they receive, and how much political representation an area gets. Abrams knew it was critically important to make sure that everyone was counted.

Abrams continued to collaborate with Georgia's House of Representatives as part of her work with Fair Fight.

The US Census

Being counted in the US Census helps your community to get the resources it needs. Census numbers are used by federal and state governments to decide how to spend money on things like schools, health care, and fire departments. Money also goes to Medicaid (medical aid for those who can't afford it), food assistance, housing assistance, and school lunch programs. Census numbers also determine fair political representation. For example, the Census determines how many congressional representatives each state has in the US House of Representatives.

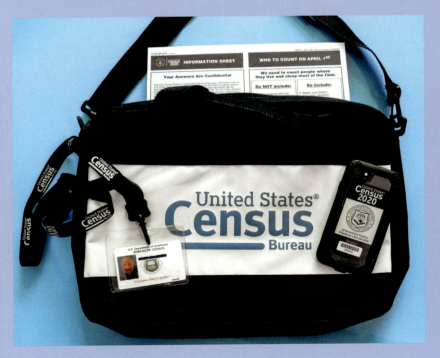

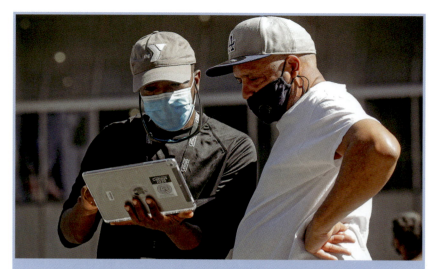

In 2020 Census workers often went door to door to collect information about American households.

The Census count is conducted through forms where people fill in information about themselves. But some may not want to give the government personal information. And some groups of people may be difficult to locate or contact. Due to concerns about communities of color, rural communities, and other historically oppressed groups being undercounted, Abrams founded Fair Count. The organization worked to ensure that these communities were counted in the 2020 Census.

In 2019 Abrams launched the Southern Economic Advancement Project to promote economic growth and prosperity in the southern US. The project focuses on improving the lives of marginalized communities in twelve southern states. Its work involves creating good jobs, supporting families, protecting the rights of workers, and offering access to better education.

A Call to Leadership

Abrams is a strong strategist and problem solver. She outlines her goals and ambitions and then creates an action plan to implement them. She asks herself three key questions: What do I want? Why do I want it? And how do I get it? She wants to end voter suppression. Daily, she takes actions to reach this goal. Her journey was documented in the film *All In: The Fight for Democracy* (2020). The film explores her 2018 campaign for governor and the work of her organization, Fair Fight. The film also puts a spotlight on voting in the US. It illustrates how tactics such as poll closures, voter intimidation, registration purges, and strict voter ID requirements suppress votes. Another tactic the film covers is gerrymandering, or the drawing of legislative districts to favor one political party over another.

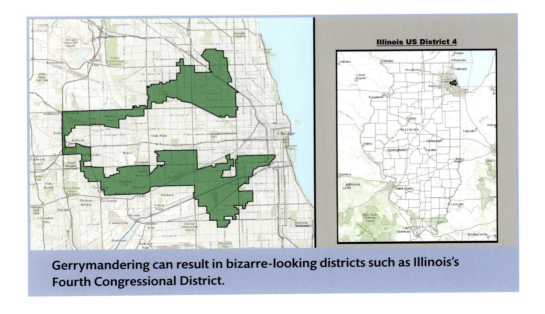

Gerrymandering can result in bizarre-looking districts such as Illinois's Fourth Congressional District.

Abrams and Senator Amy Klobuchar of Minnesota led a roundtable about voting rights in July 2021.

Finally, the film explains the need for improving the voting process and ensuring voting access for everyone.

Leaders help to build a vision for the future. They work with others who share the same values and ambitions to achieve their goals. Abrams's leadership focuses on her commitment to a strong democracy and equal voting rights. Her vision is to mobilize the collective power of ordinary people. In this vision, everyday people shape their futures through the power of the vote. "In this country, democracy is how we speak to those in power and how we determine who holds power. And that's my mission," she said.

Abrams has combined her vision with action. During her postelection speech in 2018, she said, "Put America on notice: change is not coming to Georgia. It has arrived." Through her hard work and organizing efforts, she increased voter participation and support of the Democratic Party in Georgia. Many southern states are represented mostly by Republicans. But in 2020, Abrams worked to register record numbers of voters in Georgia and across the nation. She used a boots-on-the-ground approach to organize volunteers, who in turn inspired people to get registered to vote. In Georgia more than eight hundred thousand new voters registered. Perhaps as a result, Democrats greatly increased their representation in Georgia's government. Two Georgia Democrats, the Reverend Raphael Warnock and Jon Ossoff, were elected US senators. And for the first time in more than twenty

New registered voters helped elect two Georgia Democrats to the US Senate. On January 20, 2021, Raphael Warnock (*left*) and Jon Ossoff (*second from right*) were sworn in.

Stacey Abrams in 2021

years, a Democratic presidential candidate won Georgia's electoral votes. Many credit Abrams's leadership for these historic achievements.

Many wonder what's next for Abrams. She is a dynamic, zealous advocate for justice and a globally recognized leader. In 2021 she was nominated for the Nobel Peace Prize for promoting nonviolent change through voting and civic engagement. She is the award-winning author of eight romantic suspense novels, with total sales of more than one hundred thousand copies. Her most recent book, *While Justice Sleeps*, is a legal thriller. Abrams is also an entrepreneur who creates businesses to address social challenges. She is the cofounder of Now, a financial services company that focuses on helping small businesses grow. In every part of her career, she uses her creativity and critical-thinking skills to address complex challenges.

The Nobel Peace Prize

From 1901 to 2020, 603 Nobel Prizes have been awarded to exceptional people around the world. Nobel Prizes are awarded in six categories: physics, chemistry, medicine, literature, economic sciences, and peace. The Nobel Peace Prize has been awarded to leaders such as US president Barack Obama and Liberian president Ellen Johnson Sirleaf, the first female elected head of state in Africa. It is intended to recognize efforts to increase peace by reducing armed conflict, encouraging cooperation between nations, promoting human rights, and more.

Each day, Abrams helps to write a new chapter in the history of the United States. Her dream is to lead the US as president. In an interview, she said that she hopes to become president by 2040. Meanwhile, she will keep making history and fighting for liberty and justice for all.

IMPORTANT DATES

1973   Stacey Abrams is born on December 9 in Madison, Wisconsin.

1991   She graduates from high school as her class's valedictorian.

1992   She joins a student protest at the Georgia State Capitol to speak against the use of the Confederate emblem on the state flag.

1995   She graduates with honors from Spelman College.

1998   She earns a master's degree from the Lyndon B. Johnson School of Public Affairs at the University of Texas at Austin.

1999   She graduates from Yale Law School and becomes a tax attorney.

2002   She is appointed deputy city attorney of Atlanta.

2007   She begins to serve in the Georgia House of Representatives.

2013   She creates the New Georgia Project, a voter registration organization. The nonprofit helps more than two hundred thousand community members register to vote between 2014 and 2016.

2017   She makes history when she launches her campaign for governor of Georgia.

2018   She founds Fair Fight Action, a national voting rights organization, in Georgia.

2019   She launches the Southern Economic Advancement Project to promote economic growth and prosperity in the southern US.

2020   She founds Fair Count to ensure that communities of color, rural populations, and other marginalized groups are accurately counted in the 2020 Census.

2021   She is nominated for the Nobel Peace Prize for her work in promoting voting and civic engagement.

SOURCE NOTES

11 Gregory Krieg, "Stacey Abrams Says 'Democracy Failed' Georgia as She Ends Bid for Governor," CNN, November 17, 2018, https://www.cnn.com/2018/11/16/politics/stacey-abrams -concession/index.html.

14 Ariel Goronja, "Stacey Abrams' Parents: 5 Fast Facts You Need to Know," Heavy.com, February 5, 2019, https://heavy.com /news/2019/02/stacey-abrams-parents-mom-dad-family/.

18–19 Michelle Darrisaw and Samantha Vincenty, "14 Things to Know about Stacey Abrams," Oprahdaily.com, November 6, 2020, https://www.oprahdaily.com/life/a24749080/stacey-abrams -georgia-governor-race-condede/.

19–20 Amelia Poor, "One-on-One with Stacey Abrams," Scholastics. com, May 17, 2019, https://kpcnotebook.scholastic.com/post /one-one-stacey-abrams.

21 Stacey Abrams, *Lead from the Outside: How to Build your Future and Make Real Change* (New York: Picador, 2018), 8.

25 "Stacey Abrams Tells Oprah Winfrey 'Losing Prepares You for Success': Watch News Videos Online," Global News, November 1, 2018, https://globalnews.ca/video/4619942/stacey-abrams-tells -oprah-winfrey-losing-prepares-you-for-success.

38 Adelle M. Banks, "Stacey Abrams' Zeal for Voting Began with Preacher Parents," Associated Press, October 17, 2020, https:// apnews.com/article/race-and-ethnicity-religion-stacey-abrams -georgia-voting-rights-9bef13d7118801d8adc9055a33ac1a76.

38 "Full Speech: Stacey Abrams Ends Candidacy for Georgia Governor," YouTube video, 12:01, posted by NBC News, November 16, 2018, https://www.youtube.com/watch?v =G1YXTP7u8Ds.

SELECTED BIBLIOGRAPHY

Associated Press. "What Are Voting-Rights Advocate Stacey Abrams's Plans for 2022?" MarketWatch. Updated April 23, 2021. https://www.marketwatch.com/story/what-are-voting-rights-advocate-and-nobel-peace-prize-nominee-stacey-abramss-plans-for-2022-01619044105.

Aviles, Gwen. "Stacey Abrams Has Been Fighting Voter Suppression for Years." *Harper's Bazaar*, November 6, 2020. https://www.harpersbazaar.com/culture/politics/a34599550/stacey-abrams-facts/.

Garcia-Navarro, Lulu. "A Constitutional Quirk Inspired Stacey Abrams' New Thriller, 'While Justice Sleeps.'" NPR, May 9, 2021. https://www.npr.org/2021/05/09/994605989/a-constitutional-quirk-inspired-stacey-abrams-new-thriller-while-justice-sleeps.

History.com editors. "Jim Crow Laws." History.com, March 26, 2021. https://www.history.com/topics/early-20th-century-us/jim-crow-laws.

Krieg, Gregory. "Stacey Abrams Says 'Democracy Failed' Georgia as She Ends Bid for Governor." CNN, November 17, 2018. https://www.cnn.com/2018/11/16/politics/stacey-abrams-concession/index.html.

"Stacey Abrams for Governor." Join Stacey Abrams. Accessed July 18, 2021. https://staceyabrams.com/.

"Stacey Abrams Spoke in 1993 at the Anniversary of the March on Washington." NowThis News. Accessed July 18, 2021. https://nowthisnews.com/videos/politics/stacey-abrams-spoke-at-the-anniversary-of-the-march-on-washington.

"Stacey Abrams: 'The Anguish Is Real' | Where Do We Go from Here?" YouTube video, 2:29. Posted by OWN, June 9, 2020. https://www.youtube.com/watch?v=m_QTi6ir_Hw.

Taylor, Jessica. "Stacey Abrams Says She Was Almost Blocked from Voting in Georgia Election." NPR, November 20, 2018. https://www.npr.org/2018/11/20/669280353/stacey-abrams-says-she-was-almost-blocked-from-voting-in-georgia-election.

Webster, Emma Sarran. "Stacey Abrams, Candidate to Become Georgia's Governor, Talks Fear, Failure, and Power." *Teen Vogue*, May 2, 2018. https://www.teenvogue.com/story/stacey-abrams-candidate-to-become-georgias-governor-talks-fear-failure-and-power.

LEARN MORE

Bartoletti, Susan Campbell. *How Women Won the Vote: Alice Paul, Lucy Burns, and Their Big Idea*. New York: HarperCollins, 2020.

Chambers, Veronica. *Finish the Fight! The Brave and Revolutionary Women Who Fought for the Right to Vote*. New York: Versify, 2020.

Kiddle: Stacey Abrams Facts for Kids
https://kids.kiddle.co/Stacey_Abrams

Library of Congress: The Right to Vote
https://www.loc.gov/classroom-materials/elections/right-to-vote/

Stacey Abrams
https://kids.britannica.com/kids/article/Stacey-Abrams/633174

Tyner, Artika R. *Black Voter Suppression*. Minneapolis: Lerner Publications, 2021.

INDEX